YORK NOTES

BIRDSONG

SEBASTIAN FAULKS

NOTES BY JULIE ELLAM

 Longman   York Press

YORK PRESS
322 Old Brompton Road, London SW5 9JH

PEARSON EDUCATION LIMITED
Edinburgh Gate, Harlow,
Essex CM20 2JE, United Kingdom
Associated companies, branches and representatives throughout the world

First published 2009

10 9 8 7 6 5 4

ISBN 978–1–4082–1727–6

Phototypeset by Pantek Arts Ltd, Maidstone, Kent
Printed in China (EPC/04)

CONTENTS

PART ONE

INTRODUCTION

STUDYING NOVELS

Reading novels and exploring them critically can be approached in a number of ways, but when reading the text for the first time it is a good idea to consider some, or all, of the following:

- **Format and style**: how do novels differ from other genres? How are chapters or other divisions used to reveal information? Is there a **narrator**, and if so, how does he or she convey both his or her emotions and those of the characters?

- **The writer's perspective**: consider what the writer has to say, how he or she presents a particular view of people, the world, society, ideas, issues, etc. Are, or were, these views controversial?

- **Shape and structure**: explore how the **narrative** of the story develops – the moments of revelation and reflection, openings and endings, conflicts and resolutions. Is there one main plot or are there multiple plots and sub-plots?

- **Setting**: where and when is the novel set? How do the locations shape or reflect the lives and relationships of the characters? What does the setting add in terms of tone?

- **Choice of language**: does the writer choose to write formally or informally? Does he or she use different registers for characters and narrators, and employ language features such as **imagery** and **dialect**?

- **Links and connections**: what other texts does this novel remind you of? Can you see connections between its narrative, characters and ideas and those of other texts you have studied? Is the novel part of a tradition or literary movement?

- **Your perspective and that of others**: what are your feelings about the novel? Can you relate to the narrators, characters, themes and ideas? What do others say about it – for example, critics, or other writers?

These York Notes offer an introduction to *Birdsong* and cannot substitute for close reading of the text and the study of secondary sources.

 CHECK THE BOOK

Jeremy Hawthorn's *Studying the Novel* (2005), now in its fifth edition, gives literature students a comprehensive explanation of how to analyse novels.

CHECK THE BOOK

Literary Terms and Criticism (2002) by John Peck and Martin Coyle is a useful reference work that explains many key terms.

READING *BIRDSONG*

Birdsong is set mainly during the First World War and through its central character, Stephen Wraysford, the poignancy of war and the fear experienced in battle are evoked. It uses three different time frames – 1910, 1916–18 and 1978–9 – and always pulls back to the effect that the war had on Stephen and his generation and the implications this has for future generations. *Birdsong* is a **historical novel** that remembers the massive loss of lives by focusing on a relatively small number of soldiers and officers. It is his fourth novel and the second in what has been described as Faulks's French trilogy. It is preceded by *The Girl at the Lion d'Or* (1989) and followed by *Charlotte Gray* (1998). In common with these and other works, war is an ongoing interest for the author. Jules Smith has commented on the British Council's Contemporary Writers' website: 'Faulks has made war his special subject: he has edited the *Vintage Book of War Stories* as well as writing and presenting "Churchill's Secret Army", a Channel 4 series.'

War, love and the importance of remembering history are three of the significant **themes** that appear in *Birdsong* and they demonstrate the ambition of this work. As the First World War is central to the plot, these themes are inevitably connected in that the war brings about separation, death and grief and the need to remember the dead underpins the emphasis on the importance of history. This call to remember is made overt when the **narrative** moves forward to the 1970s and Stephen's granddaughter, Elizabeth Benson, is used to connect the past with a more recognisable present.

The futility of war is another primary consideration as Stephen is observed in the British trenches on the Western Front while he and his comrades endure the seemingly endless attrition. The failure of the strategists is illustrated as are the outmoded orders that led to the record number of casualties on the Somme. The inhuman conditions of the trenches are described and these descriptions are made authentic with the numerous references to the poor hygiene and terrible food. The fear the men undergo is a paramount concern and the traditional definition of cowardice is tested by the empathy Faulks ensures we as readers feel for them.

 CHECK THE BOOK

For first-hand accounts of the First World War, *Letters from a Lost Generation* (1998) is a useful starting point. This collection of letters is taken from those written between Vera Brittain, her fiancé, brother and two male friends. All four of the men were killed in the war. The book is edited by Alan Bishop and Mark Bostridge.

The role of women is a limited but important theme to consider too. Isabelle, Elizabeth and Jeanne have crucial if relatively minor parts as they allow for facets of Stephen's character that would otherwise be missing to be revealed. His passion and tenderness are shown through his relationships with Isabelle and Jeanne, and his experiences in the war are made more relevant to contemporary readers by the introduction of Elizabeth. Faulks claims that Elizabeth is also useful for showing 'gestures of love and redemption towards the past' (Introduction, p. xv).

This is predominantly a work of war literature given the shadow that is cast by the First World War over the different time frames. It also belongs at least partially to the genre of romance because of the relationship between Stephen and Isabelle. The period when they meet, in 1910, is described as a time when relationships between the sexes were formal, on the surface at least, and it is realistic that Stephen would not make his sexual attraction to Isabelle overt in public. This sense of propriety lies behind Isabelle's initial reserve at the beginning of their relationship and their affair is all the more unlikely to be long lasting because of the guilt Isabelle experiences for leaving her husband.

In context, the First World War has been a recurring subject for writers and artists throughout the twentieth and twenty-first centuries. The war poets such as Wilfred Owen, Siegfried Sassoon and Rupert Brooke are often turned to as examples of writers who captured the mood and events that they found themselves caught up in. More recently, novels such as *Regeneration* (1992), *The Eye in the Door* (1993) and *The Ghost Road* (1995), which comprise Pat Barker's trilogy set in this era, and Sebastian Barry's *A Long, Long Way* (2005) demonstrate that a literary interest in this period continues over ninety years later. In drama, George Bernard Shaw's *Heartbreak House* (1919) and Joan Littlewood's *Oh! What a Lovely War* (1965) are just two examples of anti-war plays. More recently, the television series *Blackadder Goes Forth* (1989), by Richard Curtis and Ben Elton, uses satire to point up the inadequacies of those who sent the men out to certain destruction.

In a broader sense, historical novels have continued to be popular with the reading public. Such fictionalising of the past appears to

CHECK THE POEM
Wilfred Owen's 'Dulce Et Decorum Est' is perhaps one of the best known of the poems associated with the First World War. It describes the effects of a gas attack on the trenches. The title and last lines of the poem are used **ironically** as they declare how sweet and right it is to die for one's country.

feed an appetite for a rediscovery of history in these recreated worlds. Works such as Ian McEwan's *Atonement* (2001), which has the Second World War at its core, achieved best-selling status nationally and internationally, and novels by authors such as Kate Mosse and Philippa Gregory are regularly counted in the top-ten sales lists. This ties in with a resurgence in interest in history generally as has been seen in the popularity of television programmes such as Simon Schama's *A History of Britain* (2000).

In his Introduction, Faulks explains that at the time of writing *Birdsong* he thought that novels about the First World War tended to be 'disappointing' or mainly focused on the experiences of officers (p. xi). There are exceptions to this worth investigating, such as *Her Privates We* (1930) by Frederic Manning. Furthermore, accounts such as *Testament of Youth* (1933) by Vera Brittain give a contemporary response to the despair felt by one who has grieved for this lost generation of young men. With *Birdsong* the roles of the ordinary soldiers and the tunnellers that assisted them are given considerable space.

CHECK THE BOOK

To find out more about representations of the First World War in fiction, see *The Great War in British Literature* (2000) by Adrian Barlow.

The importance of looking back to history is key to our experience as readers of *Birdsong* and to the relevance of the novel. By forcing us to examine the full horror of the conditions that were endured on the front line, and presenting us with aspects of the war that have not been so widely documented, Faulks urges us to not forget the sacrifices these men made. As readers, the study of any literary work requires knowledge of context, of when the novel is set and written, and the **genre** or genres it is seen to belong to, as well as an understanding of the form and the content. Once armed with such knowledge, your personal interpretations and independent thinking will lead you to many interesting discoveries about a work that is rich in both personal **narratives** and historical perspectives.

PART TWO

THE TEXT

NOTE ON THE TEXT

Birdsong was first published in the United Kingdom in hardback in 1993. As Faulks describes in his Introduction to the Vintage edition, it was not published in the United States until 1996 because it took nearly three years to find 'a taker' (p. xvii). Since its release, it has been a phenomenal success in terms of sales – 2 million copies have been sold in the UK, and 3 million internationally – but there were no indicators in the early stages that the novel would be welcomed in this way: 'There were some encouraging letters from readers, some newspaper reviews (varied in response and intrinsic interest), but nothing else; it appeared on no bestseller list, nor on the numerous long and short lists compiled by that year's literary prize judges' (p. xviii).

The edition used for these Notes was first published in 1994 by Vintage; it includes an Introduction by Sebastian Faulks that was written in 2004. Here, he explains his writing process and reveals that he wrote it in 'a sort of frenzy' (p. xvi). He also outlines some of the research that he undertook for this work.

SYNOPSIS

This novel is divided into seven main parts and has the First World War, and specifically the war on the Western Front, as its main backdrop. It begins in 1910 in northern France and switches forward intermittently to England in 1978 and 1979, but the threat of impending war and the fallout from it are significant elements in these sections too. The epigraph is by Rabindranath Tagore and, as Faulks explains, was quoted by Wilfred Owen in his last letter to his mother (p. xvii).

The central **protagonist** is Stephen Wraysford who is a young Englishman. The novel begins in 1910 in Amiens, in northern France, at the point when Stephen has come to lodge with the

 CHECK THE NET
The official Sebastian Faulks website gives authorised details about his biography, books and frequently asked questions. To read this, go to **www.sebastian faulks.com**

CONTEXT
The Western Front stretched over 720 km and cut through Belgium and northern France.

Azaire family. Azaire is a factory owner involved in the textile industry and Stephen has been sent there by his employer to find out more about the manufacturing process. There is a slowly developed examination of Stephen's interest in and eventual affair with Azaire's wife, Isabelle. Compared to later parts of the novel Part One is relatively leisurely in the way events unfold, matching the pace at which the couple come together.

The backdrop of the Somme invites us to make a connection between this apparently idyllic time and the forthcoming war. This is made explicit when Stephen joins the Azaires and the Bérards on a visit to the Somme water-gardens. The conflict in the relationship between Azaire and Isabelle disrupts the idea that this is a time of peace. Their marriage is unhappy and Stephen hears the violence that Azaire inflicts on Isabelle. Unrest is also referred to in the strike of the dyers and the threat that this may spread among all the workers in the textile industry.

Part One draws to a close with Stephen and Isabelle running away together and Isabelle discovering she is pregnant. She does not tell Stephen about the pregnancy and instead returns to Rouen. She gives him no explanation as to why she has left.

Part Two leaps from this pre-war life and begins in 1916 beneath a battlefield in France. It focuses initially on Jack Firebrace and other minor characters as they create a tunnel under no-man's-land. The work of these tunnellers is drawn from fact; it is a key aspect of these war sections. Stephen is reintroduced to us as Lieutenant Wraysford. His friend, Captain Weir, and Captain Gray play significant roles in this and later war sections.

Faulks's description of the build-up to, and action on, the first day of the Battle of the Somme is one of the key features of this section and the novel as a whole. This includes a detailed examination of the unbearable tension experienced by the men as they try to prepare themselves to go 'over the top' to attack the enemy. There is a replication on a micro-scale of the chaos and carnage that took place during the day as men are shot before they even step across no-man's-land.

CONTEXT

In the Introduction, Faulks explains that he was inspired by a book that discusses the tunnelling under no-man's-land and by a story of a canary that 'had to be carried back to the surface by an officer with a phobia of birds' (p. x).

In Parts Three, Five and Seven, the **narrative** moves forward to 1978 and 1979 but is connected to the war through the character of Elizabeth Benson. It is revealed gradually that she is the granddaughter of Stephen: her increasing interest in discovering more about him and the war is used to hold the novel together. Because of her research, she represents the importance of remembering the war dead in contemporary times; when she becomes pregnant, she **symbolises** hope for the future through regeneration. When compared to Isabelle, she is an independent woman – she is the managing director of a company. However, her affair with Robert, who is a married man, has meant that she has been restricted to seeing him when he is free, thus comprising her image of independence.

Parts Two, Four and Six are set on the Western Front and include graphic descriptions of the conditions of the trenches and tunnels on the British line. Friendships that form between the men are elemental to these sections as is the grief that is brought about with the loss of loved ones.

Part Four is notable because Stephen sees Jeanne, Isabelle's sister, when on leave in Amiens. Through Jeanne, he is briefly reunited with Isabelle. Stephen later goes on to form a relationship with Jeanne.

Part Six culminates with Jack and Stephen trapped underground after an explosion: the fear of death is an overriding **theme**. After Jack dies from his injuries, Stephen is rescued by Levi, Lamm and Kroger, who are German soldiers. Thus we can see the war from the enemy perspective and witness their humanity. The episode makes it explicit that these men are not the monsters they have been constructed to be. Stephen's rescue coincides with the end of the war and Jack is buried alongside Levi's brother to commemorate this. Stephen is last seen walking back across no-man's-land to what was the British line. The sound of a lark singing is described.

The novel ends in 1979. Elizabeth is told by her mother that her grandmother was Isabelle, and not Jeanne as she had been led to believe. This final section is also concerned with Elizabeth as she gives birth to a son. She names him John in memory of Jack's son and the promise Stephen made to Jack before he died. When her partner, Robert, goes into the garden he hears the sound of a crow.

CHECK THE BOOK
Susan Hill's *Strange Meeting* (1971) gives a useful depiction and, therefore, a comparison with *Birdsong* of the isolation felt by men serving in the war.

DETAILED SUMMARIES
PART ONE: FRANCE 1910

PAGES 1–17

- Young Englishman Stephen Wraysford has come to Amiens to learn more about the textile industry and is staying with the Azaire family.
- Monsieur Azaire owns two textile factories, is a councillor and, it is implied, beats his wife.
- Stephen finds Madame Azaire attractive.
- Stephen has a notebook which he uses as a diary. He writes in code for sensitive subjects.

The novel begins in Amiens in 1910 when Stephen Wraysford, aged 20, has come to stay with the Azaires to learn more about the manufacturing process in the textile industry. The household consists of Monsieur and Madame Azaire (Isabelle) and their two children, Lisette and Grégoire.

At dinner, Stephen listens to Azaire and Lisette talk; he notices that Azaire smiles for the first time when the Bérards pay a visit. Monsieur Bérard dominates the conversation and tells Azaire his dyers (in Azaire's factories) plan to go on strike.

When Isabelle comments on a beautiful piece of music she has heard, Bérard attempts to belittle her, but she puts him aside with a look. Stephen admires this and cannot believe she is the mother of Lisette and Grégoire.

Bérard then announces unexpectedly that he will sing. He does so promptly and stares at Isabelle throughout. She looks down and the others are also embarrassed to varying degrees. Afterwards, Bérard suggests that they all play cards, but Isabelle declines by saying she has a headache and is going to bed. Stephen thinks he sees a look of complicity pass between Azaire and Bérard when Azaire says he has learned to live with her little ways; and again, later, when Azaire says he will see his wife in a while.

CONTEXT

In the period leading up to the First World War there were many examples of civil unrest in countries throughout Europe as working men and women challenged oppression. The events in Russia, which culminated in the revolution of 1917, are a prime example of this.

When the Bérards have left and Stephen is sitting in his room with his notebook, he hears a woman's voice and goes downstairs to investigate. He then hears a sob and pleading; he is sure this is Isabelle. Her voice is cut short by the sound of a thud. Stephen returns to his room when Azaire asks if anyone is there. Stephen reads his diary entry, and is surprised he has not written about that which has struck him most.

? QUESTION
How useful are Stephen's notebooks in linking the past to the present? Think about how they are used later in the novel as well.

COMMENTARY

The novel is written in the third person and this first section of Part One introduces Amiens, Stephen and the Azaires in 1910. Stephen's presence allows for an outsider's view of the family, the house and the area in this and later sections. His early role as an observer is emphasised with the references to how he has kept a notebook for five years and uses it as a diary. He writes in Greek and Latin as a form of code, and this also demonstrates his level of education, his secrecy and a wish to record what he has seen.

The context of the period just prior to the First World War is a central theme throughout Part One. It is peacetime and the several references that are made to the birds that can be heard outside the house constitute allusions to the relative calm and to the title. It also suggests the poignancy of the tragedy that is to come. When Stephen unpacks his trunk, for example, blackbirds can be heard outside: 'It was a spring evening with a late sun in the sky beyond the cathedral and the sounds of blackbirds from either side of the house' (p. 4).

The narrative avoids making the distinction between war and peace too simplistic, however, because we later learn Stephen has a phobia about birds. This is made evident in his nightmare and in his explanation to Isabelle (p. 112). This aspect of his characterisation means the title of the novel has an ironic twist: for Stephen the sound of birds denotes terror rather than peace.

Faulks's description of the house highlights that it is both intimidating with its 'formidable front door' and at the same time it has a mysterious quality: 'Inside, the house was both smaller and larger than it looked' (p. 4). Because of this air of mystery, it is depicted as unknowable; in some ways it is a metaphor for the way Stephen thinks of Isabelle, as well as being an emblem of Azaire's prosperity.

These early stages of the novel give the build-up to the later relationship between Stephen and Isabelle. It has been implied at different intervals that he is attracted to her, as when he admires her for putting Bérard aside with a look and is amazed that she is the mother of Lisette and Grégoire. Despite this apparent attraction, he does not intervene between the husband and wife when it is suggested that Azaire beats Isabelle. This may be interpreted as being an aspect of Stephen's passivity as an observer, or indifference, but it may also serve to confirm the power Azaire has in his private sphere.

The tension between the husband and wife permeates the atmosphere of the house. Whereas Azaire is **characterised** as one concerned with business and control, Isabelle is described as being cultured and easily captivated and affected by the music that she has heard in the street. The difference between them is reinforced by Bérard's presence: his bullying manner echoes Azaire's. This is made more clear when Stephen perceives the looks that pass between the two men: 'For a moment Stephen thought he had seen another half-glance of complicity between the two men, but when he looked at Bérard his face was absorbed in the cards that were fanned out in his hands' (p. 14).

Azaire's **patriarchal** influence is demonstrated in his claim that he will sack his workers rather than have them go on strike. He treats his workers and Isabelle with the same heavy-handedness, and this shows his desire to rule in both public and private spheres. His friendship with Bérard emphasises this as he appears to have more loyalty to another patriarch than he does to his wife.

? QUESTION
How does the friendship between Azaire and Bérard inform our understanding of these two characters?

GLOSSARY

7	**syndicate**	in this instance, syndicate refers to a trade union
9	**nocturne**	a lyrical piece of music associated with the evening (nocturnal)
10	**Marseillaise**	the French national anthem
11	**dewlaps**	loose skin hanging from the neck
11	**refrain**	a recurring part of a song

- Stephen visits Azaire's factory. His thoughts drift to Isabelle when Azaire and Meyraux discuss the workers' pay.
- Stephen writes about Isabelle in his coded notebook.
- On the third day of eating at the factory, Stephen rushes out and says he will not go back into the refectory.
- When the Bérards visit, Stephen notices Bérard's dominance of the conversation.
- Alone with Isabelle in the garden, Stephen takes her hand in his.

The day after hearing the mysterious noises in the Azaires' bedroom, Stephen puts the events out of his mind and goes on a tour of one of Azaire's factories. While there, Azaire brings in the syndicate leader, Meyraux, and they discuss the workers' pay, with Azaire wanting to cut it. Stephen's thoughts drift and he thinks mainly of Isabelle. The **narrative** then shifts to how he describes her and his feelings for her in a single word, 'pulse', in his coded notebook (p. 22).

A week later, when eating with the workers in the refectory of Azaire's factory, Stephen rushes out and says he feels faint. The following day Azaire asks him about this with some amusement and Isabelle tells him to leave Stephen alone. The Bérards visit after dinner and Stephen notices how Bérard conducts everyone in the room like an orchestra and cuts Isabelle off when she veers from his conversation.

One day, on Stephen's return from work, he finds her in the garden and offers to help her prune the roses. As they talk, she explains she is the stepmother of the children and has been married to Azaire for six years. The conversation ends with Stephen taking her hand in his. She asks him not to and reminds him of her position.

COMMENTARY

Azaire's dominance is reiterated here as Stephen is given a tour of his factory and made privy to Azaire's conversations with Meyraux,

CONTEXT

In 1804, Napoleon Bonaparte declared himself Emperor of France. He is considered to be one of the most influential military leaders in history. The battles of Wagram and Borodino (p. 29) were notable but costly victories for the French in the Napoleonic wars.

who is the representative of the interests of the workers. Azaire is depicted as one who is determined to cut their wages and uses the argument that this is because rationalisation is needed, which Meyraux disputes. Azaire's bullying nature and desire for control is further noticeable at the dinner table over a week later when he asks Stephen why he rushed out of the refectory, and appears to be amused that Stephen felt faint.

Azaire's power is challenged when Isabelle tells him to leave Stephen alone, and he is momentarily taken aback: 'For a moment his face had an expression of panic, like that of the schoolboy who suffers a sudden reverse and can't understand the rules of behaviour by which his rival has won approval' (p. 25). This reference demonstrates a vulnerability that has so far been disguised by brashness. His fear of loss of power is evident when he asserts himself again and tries to demean her when he asks if she has heard her 'minstrel' in her 'wanderings' in town (p. 25).

QUESTION
To what extent do Azaire and Isabelle conform to their assigned gender roles? Bear in mind how masculinity has been traditionally associated with more active roles and femininity with passivity.

Azaire's fear of losing control to Isabelle is mirrored in Bérard's treatment of her. This is most notable in his attempts to control the conversations when he visits and in the way he all but silences her when she moves away from the subject he has designated. The relationship between Bérard, Azaire and Isabelle is one that is caught up in a tension of sexual politics and a male fear of loss of masculinity. Both Bérard and Azaire are seen to be incapable of submitting to her and, instead, attempt to oppress her with words and actions. However, when Stephen attempts to defend her after she has defended him for feeling faint at the factory, she laughs at his joke, which is at the expense of the absent Bérard, and the cracks in Azaire's dominance are exposed once more.

Stephen's growing attraction to Isabelle becomes increasingly apparent. On pages 22–3, his awareness of her routines and the way she moves is detailed and he even notices how she eats and drinks: 'Her white hands seemed barely to touch the cutlery when they ate at the family dinner table and her lips left no trace of their presence on the wine glass' (p. 22). He also sees that her 'obvious strength of character overpowered conventional prettiness', but he makes no conscious judgement of how attractive she is as he is 'motivated by compulsion' (p. 28).

The element of suppressed emotions is connected to Isabelle's position as a bourgeois woman in this formal period of 1910 and Stephen's attempt to get closer to her at the end of the second section highlights why she acts with restraint. The language reiterates this formality and in these early sections – before Stephen has a relationship with Isabelle – she is referred to as Madame Azaire. This is echoed when Isabelle greets Stephen formally as 'Monsieur' on his return from work (p. 28). When she asks him to 'respect [her] position' (p. 30), presumably as the dutiful wife of a respected man, she is seen to react in accordance with her social standing.

It is telling that Stephen thinks Isabelle offers little in the way of resistance when he takes her hand as if proving that beneath the propriety she is the 'pulse' he has secretly described (p. 22). It is worthwhile remembering, however, that these thoughts come from Stephen's perspective, as they are taken from his point of view (written in the third person), whereas little direct insight is given into her emotions. There is the suggestion that she will succumb to him, as she shakes her head 'as though in defiance of some unwanted feeling', but the use of 'as though' means that her feelings for him are still unclear (p. 30).

> **? QUESTION**
> What are the connotations of Stephen's description of Isabelle as 'pulse'? Consider, for example, how this makes her appear life-affirming, close to nature, and necessary to him.

GLOSSARY

20	retrench	to reduce
23	parquet	parquet flooring is made up of small blocks of wood
30	acquiescence	the act of submitting to the authority of another without raising objections

PAGES 31–47

- Stephen discovers that Isabelle gives food to the families of the men who are on strike.
- Isabelle's background is explained.
- Stephen joins the Azaires and Bérards on a trip to the water-gardens.
- Stephen has a recurring dream of attempting to free a bird, and then being surrounded by starlings, who threaten to attack.

Stephen is dining in a café when he sees Isabelle pass the window. He rushes out to catch up with her and reaches her as she rings the bell of an unfamiliar house. They are both invited in by a man who introduces himself to Stephen as Lucien Lebrun, the man thought to be behind the dyers' strike. Lebrun refers to the strike, and Isabelle explains to Stephen that she brings food occasionally and Monsieur Lebrun gives it to a family of one of the striking men. She adds that her husband does not know about this, and that the dyers on strike are not employed by him. Stephen is concerned only about the familiarity between her and Lebrun.

> **? QUESTION**
> How does the information about Isabelle's background colour our view of her?

The **narrative** switches and gives an extensive elaboration of Isabelle's background. Her love for her older sister Jeanne is recounted as is the way Jeanne taught her to think independently. We are also told that Isabelle is the youngest of five girls and that her father thought of her as a disappointment because he wanted a son. He was a lawyer and remained distant from his family, but intervened in a long courtship she had with Jean, 'a young infantry officer' (p. 36). Her father's interference led Jean to break off the relationship and '[f]or three years her loss coloured every moment of her day' (p. 37). Her father introduced her to Azaire when she was 23.

We learn that her marriage to Azaire lacks in intimacy and he has become frustrated that she has not conceived. She has become 'less concerned' about him as time passes and is 'frightened' of Stephen because she has never met a man like him (p. 39).

The focus moves back to Stephen on a Sunday morning as he looks at the small carving he has made of a woman (and which he gives to Lisette later that day). He is asked to join the family and the Bérards on a trip to the water-gardens and he agrees to go along.

These gardens are described as being formed by 'the backwaters of the Somme' and the small islands have been cultivated (p. 42). The place is thought of with 'civic pride' and on the boat Bérard explains the history of the area as he punts them along (p. 42). Stephen is uncomfortable because of the heat and because he is seated opposite Isabelle and attempts to avoid touching her. They return to the boat and Stephen is 'repelled' by the 'stagnation' of the gardens. Isabelle's foot touches his leg; neither moves (pp. 44–5).

Once back at home, Stephen takes a cold bath and immerses himself in it. In his room later, he takes out his playing cards and uses them to tell his fortune, 'half smiling to himself, half in earnest', and it is explained that he learned to do this as a child (p. 47). He falls asleep to the sound of birds and has a variation of a recurring dream: in it he tries to let a trapped bird out of a window, but the room fills with starlings and they bring their beaks towards his face.

COMMENTARY

The background given to Isabelle's childhood and her marriage indicates how she has been suppressed first by her father and then her husband. We are told that as a child she had an 'exceptionally sweet nature' and did not question the 'indifference' of her parents (p. 35). Despite this **patriarchal** influence, she is also **characterised** as one who does not accept her fate willingly: this is apparent in her transgression when she visits Lebrun to give food to families of striking men. These men are not employed by her husband, but by giving assistance to workers on strike she challenges his political position and refuses to conform to his beliefs. Her secrecy demonstrates, however, that her rebellion is constrained by fear of reprisals.

This repressed aspect of Isabelle's character is evident in other details that are given. Faulks's description of her relationship with her closest sister, Jeanne, as she was growing up gives us an insight into how she has been introduced to ideas of freedom and female liberation. This comes most notably when Jeanne explained that menstruation (or 'blood') should not be thought of as 'shameful' (p. 35). However, it is of interest that the term blood rather than menstruation is used, implying that there is still an element of repression in her attitude to bodily functions which has not disappeared. At the time Jeanne told her this, she appreciated this information 'because it spoke of some greater rhythm of life that would lead them away from the narrow boredom of childhood', but until Stephen comes to stay she has largely behaved according to the will of others (p. 35). His appearance in the household has unsettled the life she has become used to. Isabelle's fear of Stephen is related to how different he is to other men she has encountered. It is also implied that he embodies the freedom she began to hope

CHECK THE POEM

In Samuel Taylor Coleridge's narrative poem, 'The Rime of the Ancyent Marinere' (1798), an albatross plays a pivotal role in the fate of the **protagonist** – he shoots the bird and his fellow sailors hang it round his neck as a visual **metaphor** of the burden of guilt he carries.

for as a child because he represents something different to the narrow life she leads as an adult.

The subject of a stagnant marriage is continued **metaphorically** in Stephen's view of the water-gardens: 'What was held to be a place of natural beauty was a stagnation of living tissue which could not be saved from decay' (p. 44). He is repelled by the death that surrounds him, as is made apparent in the references to the rotting vegetables and heat. Stephen's opinion of the place echoes Isabelle's relationship with Azaire as the superficial harmony is undercut by the reality of discord and decay. These negative connotations may also be interpreted as signs of how the relationship between Isabelle and Stephen is doomed, and how all of those present will inevitably die in the future: 'The tenderest parts of her that his imagination shamelessly embodied, even these would not outlast or rise above some forlorn, unspiritual end in the clinging earth' (p. 46).

In addition, the water-gardens are significant as they are 'formed by the backwaters of the Somme' and we as modern-day readers associate them with their historical context of the infamous battleground of the First World War (p. 42). Because Stephen comes to regard them as being associated with death, it is possible to see his view as a metaphoric use of **prolepsis** as references to the Somme are now so closely linked with the First World War and the carnage that took place there in 1916.

This area is thought of with pride in the town because the gardens have been created by the work of nature and human intervention, whereas the war was the responsibility only of humankind. Unfortunately the rottenness that Stephen perceives is one that will come to be remembered historically.

The **theme** of desire and death being intermingled is broached in this section and is made relevant as Stephen sits opposite Isabelle on the boat on the return home. As they touch each other and do not move away, his desire for her is heightened at the same time that he is caught up in thoughts of decay. For him, desire 'seemed indistinguishable from an impulse towards death' and it is possible to see that this heightens his pleasure and sense of immediate longing (p. 45).

 CHECK THE BOOK

For further information about the Battle of the Somme, see *Somme* (1983) by the military historian Lyn MacDonald. This draws on accounts by veteran British soldiers and uses evidence such as letters, diaries and interviews.

There is also a connection made in this instance between death and destiny and it is possible to see this referenced later when Stephen returns to his room and takes out his playing cards. He uses them to tell his fortune and although he is only 'half in earnest' he is, nevertheless, constructed as a character that at least half believes in destiny rather than free will (p. 47).

Stephen's dream at the end of this section similarly draws on the imagery of nature as his attempt to release a bird leads him to being set upon by a roomful of starlings. We are told this is a recurring dream and so are invited to suppose his past is more complex than has been revealed at this point. The wish to free the bird and risk punishment may also be read as a metaphor for a desire to release Isabelle from her restrictive relationship.

CHECK THE BOOK

See Sigmund Freud's *Beyond the Pleasure Principle* (1920) for a more developed understanding of the twin drives of desire and death (*eros* and *thanatos*).

GLOSSARY

39 **condescension** patronage; it may also be understood as patronising behaviour

44 **disconsolate** unhappy, unable to be comforted

45 **coagulated** usually refers to the clotting of blood

45 **frisson** a momentary sensation of excitement, of fear and/or pleasure

---

PAGES 48–62

- Stephen is asked to return to London shortly, but he does not want to go back yet.
- At a meeting at the factory, a fight breaks out. Stephen is caught up in it and he hits a man who slanders Isabelle.
- It is agreed that Stephen should work from the Azaire home after the conflict at the factory.
- Stephen and Isabelle make love passionately.
- He says he will not give their secret away.

Stephen receives a telegram from London the next day: it asks him to come back as soon as possible. In his reply, he asks to stay for another month because he needs to know more about the industrial processes and Azaire's finances. He also thinks that he wants to resolve the 'conflicting passions' he feels for Isabelle (p. 48).

At the factory, Meyraux talks to the workers and advises them to support the dyers with food and clothes but tells them not to go on strike too. Several men burst in with banners as he speaks and Lucien Lebrun is among them. He stands next to Meyraux on the stage and asks that they support his people. A man in the crowd implies Lucien is having an affair with a married woman and then refers to Stephen as 'a spy from England' (p. 50). Stephen is concerned only with the first remark and is told the rumour that Lucien is 'very good friends' with Azaire's wife (p. 50).

The crowd turns against Lucien and partly against Stephen. When Lucien is beaten, the other dyers and Stephen try to help him; Stephen hits the man who defamed Isabelle. He wonders how this happened so quickly, and how he found himself on Lucien's side.

Stephen feels ashamed of himself and remembers the promise he made to his guardian, Mr Vaughan, that he would not lose control in this way again. He writes to him and says he has fallen in love, but tears up the letter straightaway. At dinner, he agrees to stay away from the factory for a day or two because Azaire knows comments were made about him. Lisette notices the injury and he lies by saying he caught it in a spinning machine. Isabelle lets out 'a little cry' when she sees the damage and he thinks he notices a look of concern (p. 53).

The next morning Stephen works in the sitting room and has lunch with Lisette and Isabelle. In response to Lisette's question, he explains that he has a guardian rather than parents, and then says he will be returning home soon.

After lunch, Lisette leaves and Stephen pulls Isabelle to him. She goes to her room, weeps, then comes downstairs and tells him to come to the red room. After they make passionate love – in an intense, emotionally charged scene – they hear the sound of birds outside and they reassure each other that they will keep what has happened secret.

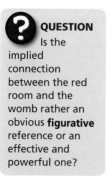

QUESTION
Is the implied connection between the red room and the womb rather an obvious **figurative** reference or an effective and powerful one?

COMMENTARY

This section is mainly significant for the scene when Stephen and Isabelle make love. The earlier parts of the novel have been building up to this: the sexual tension between them has been suggested intermittently and is brought to the fore here. Their passionate union is instigated initially by Stephen when he pulls Isabelle towards him, but is continued by her when she asks him to come to the red room.

This passage is markedly different to what has come before because of its surreal quality. When Stephen worries that he will not be able to find the room, and so follows quickly after her, it becomes reminiscent of a fairy tale: 'By the time Stephen turned round she had gone. The red room. He panicked. He was sure it would be one of those he had once seen but could never refind; it would be like a place in a dream that remains out of reach; it would always be behind him' (p. 58). The name of the room has connotations of other worldliness as well as echoes of the supernatural horror of *Jane Eyre*. Because he worries that he will not be able to find it, he also momentarily transforms into a lost child. He becomes the boy she considers him to be in this instant. This unrealistic aspect is also used to heighten the sexual **metaphors** because the red room may be interpreted as a metaphor for the womb.

The explicit sexual nature of the passage set in the red room forces us to focus on the bodies of Isabelle and Stephen. Parallels may be drawn between these references and the graphic descriptions of corpses in the sections set in the war. In sex and death, bodies are anatomised in this **narrative** and, therefore, broken down into pieces for our analysis.

The scene in the red room is also relevant for what it reveals about Isabelle's thought processes: 'She wanted him to bring alive what she had buried, and to demean, destroy her fabricated self' (p. 58). This quotation points out how she sees Stephen as her saviour, as though he will resurrect her 'true' self, and also reminds us that during her marriage she has lived a lie as she has had to construct a new persona to fit with her role as a bourgeois wife.

CHECK THE BOOK
When a child, Jane, of *Jane Eyre* (1847) by Charlotte Brontë, is sent to the red room as a punishment. This novel is also comparable to *Birdsong* for the use of an orphan (Jane) as a central **protagonist**. *The Madwoman in the Attic* (1979) by Sandra M. Gilbert and Susan Gubar offers a useful criticism of *Jane Eyre* and the **symbolic** nature of the red room.

QUESTION
In the Introduction, Faulks explains how his original title for this novel was 'Flesh and Blood' (p. xvi). Taking into account the explicit sex scenes and the depictions of mutilations and death in the war scenes, to what extent is this earlier title still relevant to the work?

We should also note that Stephen's upbringing is alluded to for the first time. He explains to Lisette and Isabelle that he is an orphan; after being cared for by grandparents and then taken to an institution he gained a guardian called Mr Vaughan. Up to this point, few details of his past have been given and it is only in this section that we learn how his shame at hitting the man in the factory is linked to a promise he made Mr Vaughan years ago that he would never lose control in this way. By only giving clues to his history rather than explaining it with direct exposition, Faulks allows Stephen to remain a mysterious figure: his past is as little known by us as it is by Isabelle.

> **GLOSSARY**
> 49 fraternity brotherhood
> 59 upbraided criticised
> 59 lambent flickering, radiant

PAGES 63–78

- Stephen reveals more details of his childhood to the Azaires.
- He notices another look of complicity pass between Bérard and Azaire with regard to Isabelle.
- Stephen visits the cathedral and envisages mass death.
- He and Isabelle make love in the red room again.
- Isabelle tells Stephen about the violence in her marriage.

CONTEXT
The total of war dead in the First World War is thought to be more than 8 million.

At dinner that night, Lisette tells Azaire that she had 'a very strange dream', but giggles and says she will not tell him when he asks what it was about (p. 63). Stephen shows remarkable control in hiding their secret from the rest of the family and Isabelle worries that he is being indifferent to her. After Azaire invites him to come with them on a fishing trip, Stephen begins to talk about when he used to fish as a child and tells them how he was ordered off private property. Isabelle is surprised at how long he talks to Azaire and is proud of him.

The narrative then shifts back and describes how Isabelle has to remove all signs of their adultery in the red room. The 'major problem' to sort out is the stained bedding and how to clean it without bringing this to the attention of Marguerite the servant. Isabelle decides to clean the sheets herself and throw the red cover away (p. 66).

The Bérards visit and after being asked if she has heard the pianist today, Isabelle tells Bérard she has been reading about a young man who 'falls in love with the wrong kind of people' (p. 67). Stephen notices how adept she is at lying and wonders if she might do the same to him in the future. He thinks that he would not know if she did. She flushes when Stephen looks at her body, and the others notice her colour. Feigning illness, she goes up to bed and Bérard winks at Azaire, who responds with a smile. Stephen goes up to her room to offer some reassurance and leaves 'soundlessly to his own ears at least' (p. 71).

The next morning Stephen goes into town. He sits in the cold cathedral, where he has something akin to a premonition of dead people piled up. He prays that he, Isabelle and everyone will be saved from it.

When he comes back home, he and Isabelle return to make love in the study, and then again in the red room. After falling asleep, they wake and Stephen broaches the subject of Azaire's violence towards her. She explains a little of the history of their troubled relationship and how she also thinks Azaire talks about her to his friends. The section ends with them sleeping again; the sound of doves can be heard outside.

COMMENTARY

The **theme** of the passing of time is often drawn upon in this section: for example, when Stephen considers if Isabelle might lie to him in the future. In contrary terms, this signals that he is at least partially considering the chance that they will have more than the present moment together. The future is also referred to when Stephen visits the cathedral and has a premonition of sorts about 'a terrible piling up of the dead' and 'the row on row, the deep rotting earth hollowed out to hold them' (p. 72). We as readers know that

 CHECK THE NET
The Commonwealth War Graves Commission has an informative website about the war dead of the Commonwealth in the First World War. It offers details about various battles, including the Battle of the Somme 1916, and photographs and maps in the 'Histories' section. This is available at **www.cwgc.org**

this refers to the forthcoming massacre of men in the First World War. There are also connections to be made with this imagery, the earlier scene at the water-gardens and the excavations made by the tunnellers on the Western Front later in the novel. Death comes to be seen by Stephen as the end of time and his prediction of the numbers of dead is later referred to as a moment of recognition explaining the change in his attitude to religion.

This reference to the vision of the dead is also a use of prolepsis as the foreshadowing of events in the novel is related. With the use of this premonition, and an expectation that we as readers will have some prior knowledge of the First World War, we are given an indication of how the war dead are to be a major focus in later sections.

The institution of religion is also a thematic concern. It is criticised by Stephen with the adjectives he uses in his view of the cathedral as 'chilly' and 'hostile' and in how he sees it as offering only 'dignity' to the 'trite occurrence of death' (p. 71). Isabelle has been brought up as a Catholic and her affair with Stephen therefore challenges her religious beliefs. However, she considers at the end of the section how although the Church would see her affair with Stephen as a sin, she feels it is right.

Stephen's vulnerability and confusion are made more evident through the figurative and literal allusions to his childhood and through the symbolism borrowed from fairy tales. His past life is described as 'a wood of confusion' and the few 'clear tracks' feel like scars that he does not want to share with others (p. 71). Although he ultimately trusts Isabelle, he does not wish to reopen these wounds. He is seen to cope with his difficulties by attempting to repress his emotions, but it is demonstrated that he is not able to do this completely.

The references to 'wood' and 'tracks' are evocative of children's stories; they also have the effect of making us imagine him as a boy who has been lost and is still afraid of this happening again. This is seen most clearly when he and Isabelle arrange to meet in the red room and once again he worries that he will not be able to find it as it might not be there. For this reason, it is possible to see that Stephen is still troubled by what has occurred in the past.

CONTEXT

The evocation of fairy tales and their associated symbols highlights how the adult Stephen has repressed his childhood memories. These allusions to the tales also bring in another narrative thread that emphasises how unreal his experiences appear to be (for him). For a detailed analysis of fairy tales, the work of Jack Zipes, such as *Fairy Tales and the Art of Subversion: The Classical Genre for Children and the Process of Civilization* (1983), is a useful starting point.

The history of the violence between Isabelle and Azaire is given some detail as she explains how the trouble between them stems from her not conceiving as he wanted her to. Isabelle tells how Azaire said she 'castrated' him and how he began by hitting her for pleasure to arouse himself and has continued ever since (p. 76).

Isabelle is also depicted as being in conflict with the expectations placed on her as a dutiful bourgeois Catholic wife, and with the reality of the unhappiness she endures for the sake of respectability: 'It's the humiliation. He makes me feel like an animal. And I feel sorry for him because he humiliates himself' (p. 77). In her description of the domestic violence she suffers Isabelle emphasises that she does not stay with Azaire because of physical fear, but rather it is because of expectations placed on a woman of this time: divorce is both against her religion and seen as scandalous.

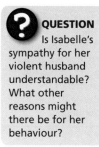

QUESTION
Is Isabelle's sympathy for her violent husband understandable? What other reasons might there be for her behaviour?

GLOSSARY

70 **pastoral** refers to country life

71 **memento mori** literally translated this means 'remember, you must die'; it also means a warning or reminder of death, often an object, such as a skull

71 **lapidary inscription** an inscription in stone

PAGES 79–88

- We learn that Azaire does not suspect Isabelle of adultery.
- Stephen joins the Azaires on a fishing trip at Beaucourt.
- Stephen knows he wants to be with Isabelle in the future, but has not thought about how this will be possible.
- Lisette tells Stephen that she knows of his affair with Isabelle and wants to have a relationship with him as well.

We learn that although Azaire does not love Isabelle, he still wants her to respond to him with affection. He does not suspect her of adultery and does not consider Stephen to be a threat to his marriage.

CONTEXT

The Albert–Bapaume road was a focal point of the July period of the Battle of the Somme.

At the weekend, Stephen joins the family on a fishing trip; they pass through Albert to reach Beaucourt. On the train journey, Lisette refers to Stephen by his first name rather than 'Monsieur Wraysford' and Isabelle reprimands her for this. Lisette is silent when Stephen turns his attention to Grégoire.

They dine at a restaurant and Stephen thinks how Isabelle was 'Madame Azaire' to him only six days ago. He gives her a look of assurance and he sees her soften. He realises he will not return to England just yet because he wants to discover where the relationship will lead.

On their return to the river, Stephen sits a short distance away from the group. He feels a hand pressed against his eye, and presumes it is Isabelle. He discovers it is Lisette who tells him that she knows he expected it to be someone else. She then reveals she knows he and her stepmother have been meeting secretly; she suggests she knows they are having an affair.

Lisette reminds Stephen that she is closer to his age than Isabelle. She also tells him that she wants to do the same with him as Isabelle does (that being, to make love with him). When he tries to dismiss this as fancy and laughs at her, she says it is not funny and attempts to blackmail him by saying if he does not do as she wishes she will tell her father. Lisette says that she thinks Stephen has led her on by giving her the wooden carving, and tells him she is a woman. She places his hand on her breast and then under her skirt and at first he is aroused. However, when he pulls his hand away she looks frightened. She agrees to say nothing about the things she knows.

COMMENTARY

Faulks's description of Lisette's feelings for Stephen – that she is a potential rival of Isabelle for his affection – and her frightened reaction when he touches her highlight how while she is not a child any more, she is not yet a woman.

This short episode also reflects how Stephen reacts instinctively rather than analytically. Faulks describes the way Stephen has lived his life up to this point and conducted his relationship with Isabelle: 'His confidence in himself was not checked by judgement;

he followed where nothing more than instinct took him, and relied on some reflexive wariness to help' (p. 85). This aspect to Stephen's character becomes more apparent later in the novel when he is serving in the war: it may be understood as a form of indifference. It also colours the feelings he has for Isabelle and the time they might have together. He has arranged with his employers to stay for another three weeks, but postpones informing her of this: 'He didn't mention the date of his departure to Isabelle; it seemed sufficiently distant for him not to have to worry, and the days were so full that his life seemed to change from one to the next' (p. 80). Here there is an emphasis on how he tries not to consider the future or look back to the past for help, and instead lives in the continuing present.

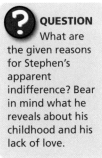

QUESTION
What are the given reasons for Stephen's apparent indifference? Bear in mind what he reveals about his childhood and his lack of love.

PAGES 89–108

- Isabelle and Stephen continue to make love in secret; he asks her to come to England.
- Isabelle admits to Azaire that she took food to the families of the striking men.
- She also admits that she has been having an affair with Stephen.
- Stephen and Isabelle leave together.
- Stephen tells her more about his childhood.

Over the next week, Stephen and Isabelle continue to make love in the red room and he tells her about Lisette's flirtatiousness and forwardness, but Isabelle is unconcerned and does not see her as a rival. They then talk of the future and how he is to leave next week. Stephen says Isabelle should come to England with him. She does not want the children to lose another mother, but he is more concerned about her well-being.

When Azaire returns from work, he tells them the strike is over and Isabelle considers how lonely she will be if she spends the rest of her life with him. Azaire then tells them that he has heard a woman has been bringing food to Lucien for the families of the striking men and that she is married to the factory owner. He says he has also heard a rumour that she has been sleeping with Lucien. Isabelle admits to helping the families and says she has been having an affair with Stephen, not Lucien.

Stephen breaks into the conversation and says that he 'seduced' her and although he feels pity for Azaire, he hardens himself 'in the interests of preserving something' for himself and Isabelle (p. 95). Azaire regains some composure and demands that Stephen leave. Stephen tells Azaire that he will go and will take Isabelle with him. Isabelle is at first undecided, but after Azaire apologises she does the same and then goes to pack. Azaire insists she will go to hell for this. He checks the rooms for signs of their adultery and forgets about the red room in his 'haste and rage' (p. 100).

Isabelle and Stephen board a train heading south and they stay at a hotel in Plombières. He goes on to tell her more about his childhood and how he came to live in an institution. He also explains how Vaughan adopted him and although he gained a good education under his care, he was not treated like a son by him.

After a week, they travel further south where Stephen finds work 'as an assistant to a furniture maker' (p. 107). He occasionally feels troubled by the closeness of Isabelle and at such times he tries to think only of the immediate present.

COMMENTARY

The **characterisation** of Stephen is given more depth in this section as he recounts to Isabelle how his father left his mother when she was pregnant and his mother abandoned him to be cared for by her parents. The necessity of being independent in his childhood and his experience of not being loved is vital to understanding his perspective as an adult when he is in the trenches. This is because the abandoned child is described as never fully recovering from the trauma. He relates the story of his life with apparent fortitude, but it is possible to see at least a suggestion of how this has affected him: 'There seemed to be no emotion in his voice, though the line of his jaw had tightened a little' (p. 103).

When Stephen describes the institution he was taken to as a child, which happened after the arrest of his grandfather, parallels may be

---

CONTEXT

Marxist theorists understand society as being divided along class lines and offer a useful framework for literature students when discussing such subjects.

drawn with this place and the army. When he looks back at this time as an adult, he experiences panic at 'being reduced to numbers, to ranks of nameless people who were not valued in the eyes of another individual' (p. 104). This language highlights a resistance to being made subservient and anonymous.

This may also be understood as a reaction against being unfairly treated because of his working-class origins. Through Stephen, it is possible to see, therefore, that the **narrative** questions the English class system where those of the lower classes have been, and still are according to a Marxist perspective, regarded as expendable and inhuman by those in a more materially secure position. By using terms such as 'numbers' and 'ranks' the criticism of the army is also made apparent.

Stephen's explanation of his mainly loveless childhood may be linked loosely to the uneasiness he feels sometimes when he lies next to Isabelle in bed. At such times, he physically removes himself and sleeps on the sofa. He cannot look beyond 'the moment and the next day': 'It was an existence he felt had been won by him but in some wider judgement would not be allowed' (p. 108). As well as referring to a superstitious belief, or a possibly religious view that they have committed a sin, this exemplifies a fatalistic approach to enjoying a loving relationship.

The idea of not understanding how to love another person is continued in the way Stephen regards Isabelle as a spoil of victory. He sees her as something won in battle, which may be connected to his treatment in the institution (which appears to have had the discipline of an army). His lack of love and consequent inability to demonstrate it are further emphasised when he explains to her that his guardian, Vaughan, never gave him the love of a father. Instead, Stephen sees him more as a 'social reformer' who helped to improve his life physically but not emotionally (p. 105).

> **CONTEXT**
>
> In Part Two we learn that Stephen has been promoted up through the ranks of the army to lieutenant by 1916 (p. 189).

GLOSSARY

97 **harlot** prostitute

107 **bourgeois opulence** middle-class signs of wealth

PAGES 109–117

- Isabelle discovers that she is pregnant; she decides not to tell Stephen.
- She has no regrets about the affair with him, but is beginning to feel guilty.
- Stephen reveals his phobia of birds to her.
- Without informing him of her decision to go or of her pregnancy, Isabelle leaves. Her concern for the well-being of the child now overrides her relationship with Stephen.

Two months pass and Isabelle is described as content and as not missing her old life. Her period has not come by January and she realises she is pregnant. Crucially, she decides not to tell Stephen. When she feels faint on a walk, he disappears to find her some smelling salts; while he is away she imagines her child as a grown man. She also considers how the other mothers in the surrounding villages have sons and how they will never meet unless there is a war. She thinks of her own family and how she would like to contact Jeanne. The guilt of the affair with Stephen is now beginning to come to the fore in her thoughts.

QUESTION
Why is Stephen's fear of birds relevant to the title?

Stephen returns with the smelling salts and some food; as they share it a pigeon sits between them. He cannot bear to have the bird so close by and trembles because of its presence. He explains to her why he has always hated birds.

A week later, Isabelle loses some blood and is afraid she is having a miscarriage. Although she has not lost the baby, she is frightened of the possibility. She writes to Jeanne to explain this and reveals that Stephen does not know about the pregnancy. Isabelle also tells her sister how Stephen is distant about his own life history and that she feels they have been 'unscrupulous' by having an affair (p. 115). Unknown to Isabelle, Stephen has been thinking of taking her to his old home in England; but, unknown to Stephen, she arranges to leave him and he realises this only once she has gone.

COMMENTARY

There is a significant use of dramatic irony in this last section of Part One, as Isabelle believes Stephen to be distant even about his own life, whereas he has been considering taking her to his grandparents' old home because he wants to share this part of his past with her now. This is because 'his life's concern' is her 'well-being' (p. 116). Ironically, it is the fear for the well-being of her child that impels her to go to Jeanne rather than stay with him.

When he discovers she has left, the effect is compared to that of a block of wood being split. This **simile** cleverly describes his emotional state because, although he shows no outward sign to his co-workers, he is ripped apart inside: 'No shred or fibre escaped the sundering' (p. 117). Further to this, blankness descends on him: 'he could think of nothing' (p. 117). In terms of his **characterisation**, Stephen is constructed as becoming numb. It is possible to see this aspect of him continued later in the trenches when he appears to be cold or indifferent.

With regard to Stephen's now evident phobia of birds, it is explained how this is related to a childhood incident when a boy whom he later fought dared him to touch a dead crow that had 'maggots under its wings' (p. 112). Stephen's violence in the fight with this boy reached the newspapers, and this is how Vaughan learned of Stephen. He also explains how he has always hated birds as there is 'something cruel, prehistoric about them' (p. 112). This fear sits ironically with the received belief that birdsong is an emblem of innocence because for Stephen it is a form of torture.

CHECK THE POEM

'My Last Duchess' (1842) by Robert Browning draws on dramatic irony to highlight the gap between appearance and reality. In the course of the poem, the speaker (the Duke of Ferrara) exposes his preference for the portrait of his dead wife over the woman she was, and in so doing his cruelty is revealed.

GLOSSARY

113 **prosaically** unimaginatively, in a dull fashion

PART TWO: FRANCE 1916

PAGES 119–44

- In France in 1916, Jack Firebrace, a tunneller, is underground.
- A letter from his wife, Margaret, tells Jack that their son is in hospital.
- On sentry duty, Jack is caught sleeping. He must report to Stephen, who is now an officer.
- Jack reports to Stephen's dugout where Stephen says he does not recall the incident and tells him he cannot charge him anyway.
- The tunnellers are relieved for a short while and are billeted in a nearby village.

Part Two begins in France in 1916. Jack Firebrace is 45 feet (15 m) underground and thinks he has been working (as a tunneller) for six hours. Faulks gives a powerful description of the almost airless conditions. Jack is asked to listen for enemy movements, and he decides the noise comes from shell fire. Shortly afterwards an attack from the enemy kills four of the men.

Jack is unscathed by the blasts and when he returns to his trench he is given a letter from his wife, Margaret. Brief details of Jack's background and that of his fellow workers Tyson and Shaw are given and the horrors of the trenches are alluded to. Despite being exhausted, Jack has to go on sentry duty, but before doing so he reads Margaret's letter which informs him that their son, John, has diphtheria.

On duty, Jack sees his son's face, then falls asleep. He is woken by Captain Weir, who commands the group of tunnellers, and another officer, and the latter accuses Jack of sleeping on duty and reminds him that this is a court-martial offence. He tells Jack to see him in his dugout at 6 am the next day. After his shift, Jack thinks about how the punishment for this offence means being shot; he cannot think of his own death without shaking.

CONTEXT

Without a vaccination, diphtheria is a life-threatening illness that affects the upper respiratory tract. Since the immunisation of children in the 1940s, it has almost been eradicated in Britain.

It is revealed that the officer is Stephen (who is referred to as Lieutenant Wraysford). When Jack reports to him the next day as requested, Stephen asks him why he has come to see him. Jack reminds him of the offence and Stephen says that there is no charge because he is not under his command.

The tunnellers are relieved from their work and sent to a billet, or lodging house, in a nearby village. On the night before they go back to the front, the men sing. Jack tells jokes, but before he reaches the end of his routine he feels dread at the thought of returning to war.

COMMENTARY

The beginning of Part Two cuts directly away from the end of Part One and, without any **exposition**, a new character, Jack Firebrace, is used as the main focus. This is disorientating for us and may be interpreted as mimicking the effects of war generally. It also highlights the specific example of what it was like to work in these tunnels. In this instance, these men are unaware of the time or place and by not revealing such details directly their experience resonates more fully. We as readers and the tunnellers are uprooted from an established environment and placed in this initially alien world.

The direct shift to the First World War also gives an air of mystery to the fate of Stephen. He is introduced only gradually as the lieutenant who causes Jack to fear the threat of a court-martial. This method allows the **narrative** to expose how others view him: for example, Sergeant Adams describes him to Jack as blowing 'hot and cold' (p. 132).

The **theme** of the mortal danger of war is encapsulated not only in Jack's belief that he is to lose his life – the probable outcome of his court-martial if it had gone ahead – but also in the tunnel at the beginning of Part Two when an explosion kills four of his colleagues. The fear that accompanies this danger is expressed when Jack considers returning to the front after a few days leave: 'The leaving of this undistinguished village now seemed to him the most difficult parting he had had to make; no sundering from parents, wife, or child, no poignant station farewell, could have been

CHECK THE BOOK

For Services Rendered (1932) by Somerset Maugham is an anti-war drama that is set after the war. It highlights the terrible legacy for those who survived and for those who were grieving.

undertaken with heavier heart than the brief march back through the fields of France' (p. 144). This fear exists despite his evident bravery. As has already been observed, he and the others work in life-threatening conditions, but the possibility of a death sentence from a court-martial still terrifies him.

This section is of importance because it introduces the work of the miners and tunnellers in the First World War. Their support of the troops is a little known fact of this war and its use by Faulks gives us something new (as he explains in the Introduction, p. xii), but is also an act of remembrance of these men who have thus far been overlooked. By the inclusion of this storyline, their history has been preserved in fiction and readers in the twenty-first century are at least made aware of the conditions they endured.

CHECK THE NET

There is a cross-section diagram of a typical British trench showing the firestep (p. 128) at **www.spartacus.schoolnet.co.uk/FWWstep.htm**

Further to this **theme**, references are made to the conditions in the trenches. They are described as cramped with hardly any room to sleep, and Jack is pictured being woken by a rat crawling across his face. That he is 'rocked between' the fear of being buried by a shell and the need to 'lose consciousness of the noise that assailed them' demonstrates the unbearable environment they inhabit (p. 125). The **image** evoked by the phrase 'rocked between' is that of a child being rocked in a cradle. Ironically, this situation is the polar opposite of the innocence associated with childhood, but it is also the place where many men call for their mothers when close to death.

This point may also be connected to a discussion of Jack's relationship with his son, John, and how it is difficult for Jack to think of him. Jack does not have a photograph of his son and it is implied that to survive the war both physically and psychologically Jack finds it problematic to consider home. The demands of war mean that his home life has taken a secondary role: 'There was always too much to think of to allow his mind to dwell on inessentials' (p. 128). The use of the word 'inessentials' in relation to his wife and son demonstrates an ambivalent attitude to what is now his former life and underlines the effect the war has had on him.

GLOSSARY

128 **firestep** a raised part of the trench that made it possible to see and fire through the parapet

129 **court-martial** the use of military law and courts to discipline those not following orders in the armed forces

141 **NCO** non-commissioned officer; an enlisted soldier who has been promoted and has authority over other enlisted men

143 **estaminet** a small café

PAGES 145–66

- Stephen's section of the line has been shelled for three days.
- Stephen and Captain Weir talk about the war and how people back home do not know how terrible it is.
- When Stephen is on leave, his thoughts turn to Amiens; some explanation is given as to what happened to him after Isabelle left.
- Captain Gray talks to Stephen and tells him he has to make his men love him.

Stephen is shattered by the three-day spell of enemy shelling, but it is his job to reassure his men even though he finds it difficult. He is seen to have problems with this partly because he was promoted from the ranks, and is therefore one of them, and also because these men have been prepared to walk into the fire of machine guns, but are understandably terrified of the damage that shells can do.

Weir comes to talk with him and to drink whisky. Stephen tells him that without his curiosity to see how far men will be pushed, he would have committed suicide by now. He then leaves for his section because his men have been hit by shells.

Stephen's company has three days' rest at Béthune and he sleeps for twelve hours. His thoughts turn to Bérard and Isabelle. It is then explained how he came to join the army. It was a relief for him when the war started and he presumed like many that it would last only a year, as the newspapers in France and Britain reported. However, once in France and fighting, he realised the impossibility of this.

 CHECK THE POEM
Henry Newbolt's poem, 'Vitae Lampada' (1897), is an example of poetry being used to glorify war; it had a resurgence in popularity in the early days of the First World War and is in sharp contrast to the anti-war poems of Owen and Sassoon.

CONTEXT

Sigmund Freud is one of the founders of psychoanalysis; he is alluded to in the reference to the Viennese school of psychiatry. Gray's interest in psychoanalysis is apparent when he discusses, later in Part Two (p. 193), Stephen's penchant for superstitions.

In the present, Stephen has breakfast with Captain Gray who is described as an avid reader of works ranging from Thomas Hardy to the Viennese school of psychiatry, as well as a strict disciplinarian.

COMMENTARY

Because Stephen is seen to have been promoted from the ranks, this part of the **narrative** is based on both an officer's experience as well as one of a working-class man who has been part of the infantry. In this way, Faulks prevents the novel being yet another First World War fiction that focuses only on the officer class. He challenges such work (which he mentions as memoirs, but does not specify the titles) in his Introduction to the novel (p. xiv) and it is telling that Stephen is used to filter the fears of the men from the ranks and the officers. The use of Jack and his colleagues adds to this well-rounded perspective of the war on the Western Front. It is not restricted in terms of rank or class.

The unnaturalness of the existence that is created by war is reiterated through Stephen. One of his earliest reactions to the fighting, after realising it would not last just a year as the newspapers claimed, is that it goes against humanity and laws of nature: 'There seemed to him a great breach of nature which no one had the power to stop' (p. 162). This reference to the contravening of expectations and humanity exemplifies how this man-made catastrophe seems to have no sign of ending. The novel captures the desperation of those caught up in it.

It is moving, and also realistic, that the areas where the men are billeted on rest days are only a few miles away from the front, but also a world away from the war. Stephen voices how civilians in England know very little about the reality of trench warfare or the conditions they endure: 'This is not a war, this is an exploration of how far men can be degraded' (p. 150). The false notions concerned with bravery and signing up to fight for King and Country are quashed by his claim that it is only curiosity that is keeping him alive. If he was not curious about how far men can be 'degraded', he says, he would have killed himself by now (p. 150).

The damage caused by shells is a recurring motif in these pages as Stephen describes the fear experienced by him and his men and, after they are hit, the injuries sustained. Half of Reeves's ribcage is missing and Wilkinson's skull has only ragged edges on one side. Further to this, Douglas's injury is so serious that when Stephen presses a dressing to his wound he feels his hand move down towards his lung. As Stephen knows, the men dread the shells more than the bullets 'because they had seen the damage they did' (p. 147).

 CHECK THE NET

In 1915, the so-called Order of the White Feather was created by Admiral Charles Fitzgerald to encourage women to hand out a white feather (a **symbol** of cowardice) to men who they thought should be fighting in the war. Find more about the campaign at **www.spartacus. schoolnet.co.uk/ FWWfeather.htm**

GLOSSARY

147 **duckboards** wooden boards used to stop the men sinking in the mud

148 **MO** Medical Officer

154 **commission** being given a commission means that the rank of officer has been conferred

161 **Territorials** the Territorial Army, a non-professional, reserve army

---

PAGES 167–84

- Weir asks Gray for more defence for his men working in the tunnels; Gray agrees and Stephen is put in charge of these soldiers.
- Stephen goes down into the tunnels and tries to quell Hunt's panic.
- Stephen is dragged out after being injured.
- Close to death, he is placed outside the medical tent.
- Jack sees Stephen is still alive and rescues him.

This section begins with Jack's request for leave being turned down and the narrative moves to the cramped conditions of the tunnels. The one Jack is working in is so confined that he and Shaw have to crawl over each other when Shaw comes to take over from Jack.

Stephen takes Hunt and Byrne down with him when they are asked to defend the tunnellers. Hunt's panic triggers Stephen's fears as he is undone by the thought of not being able to turn around. Gunfire breaks out as the Germans make their way through to the British tunnel; Stephen is shot and wounded by grenade fragments.

Stephen is dragged up to the surface and has to wait for a day to be treated because the injured are not a priority. He suffers from a fever and screams at the thought of dying alone. After being seen at the medical tent, he is left outside to either die or be taken to the casualty clearing station.

Jack goes to find out what has happened to Stephen. He is told his body is with those of the other dead and he decides to say a prayer for him. At this point, he sees Stephen, who 'loomed from the half-light towards him', and notes that he is naked apart from a boot on one foot and an identity disk around his neck (p. 180).

Meanwhile, Weir wonders about Stephen and thinks he would have heard from him by now if he were still alive. Weir thinks if Stephen is dead he will not be able to continue.

COMMENTARY

Stephen's life-threatening injuries and the consequent disposal of his body dominate these pages. His movement between yearning for oblivion and the primal fear of not wanting to die alone are emphasised: when the medical officer is told that Stephen has been shouting for his mother he replies, 'They always do' (p. 177). The impact of the war is glimpsed here in the regression that is displayed. The scene also captures how the injuries are psychological as well as physical. At what appears to be his final moment, Stephen turns back to his first love, his mother.

CHECK THE FILM

The 1930 film adaptation of Erich Maria Remarque's *All Quiet on the Western Front* (1929) depicts the disillusionment of soldiers on the front line. The film won two Oscars, for best director and best film.

Stephen's desire for love is made apparent in the descriptions of his fear of dying alone and of how he thinks of Isabelle as he believes he is 'in a house on a French boulevard in which he searched and called the name Isabelle' (p. 177). This hallucination demonstrates how ill he is, but it is also reminiscent of his time in the Azaire home when he worried that he would not be able to find the red room again. The abandoned child is now an adult but he is again seen to have never come to terms with this loss.

The emotion of primal fear is also depicted when Hunt panics in the tunnel. The claustrophobic atmosphere is emphasised as he reacts uncontrollably and says 'I'll take my chances in the trench' (p. 171). **Figuratively**, the tunnel may be interpreted as an ideal **symbol** for regression because it may be seen as a **metaphor** for the birth canal. Hunt desires to escape from it literally for safety, but also to escape this primal regression.

The shift from the scene of Stephen's apparent death to Jack deciding to pray for him has the effect of bringing these two men together. The **narrative** switches in focus from Stephen to Jack, and Jack's rescue of Stephen is a prelude to Part Six when they will be trapped in the tunnel together and Stephen will try to rescue him. It is a significant moment in the plot, then, when Jack discovers Stephen among the dead, because it underpins the later camaraderie between them.

GLOSSARY

174 camouflet a hole or crater formed by an underground explosion

184 phosgene the common name for carbonyl chloride, which is a poisonous gas used in the First World War

---

PAGES 185–212

- Stephen recovers gradually in hospital and witnesses the suffering of other patients.
- Gray presumes Stephen is interested in superstition because of childhood experiences.
- Stephen and Weir visit prostitutes.
- Jack learns of the death of his son.
- The division moves near Beaumont; the men think they are about to attack.
- Gray takes Stephen to see Colonel Barclay, who informs them he will be with them in the trenches when they go over the top.

As Stephen recovers, he sees a young man brought into the ward. He has been gassed and burned and his horrific injuries mean that

CHECK THE BOOK

We That Were Young (1932) by Irene Rathbone is an anti-war novel written from the perspective of those nursing just behind the lines.

he cannot even bear to be touched by a sheet. His agony is so great that Stephen prays for him to die.

Gray visits Stephen before he is discharged and informs Stephen that he has been given two weeks' home leave and after this he will be promoted to brigade staff. Gray is surprised when Stephen tells him he refuses both of these offers, which are orders, and that he wants to stay on the front line. Stephen shows interest, though, when told that they are being moved to Albert and the brigade staff headquarters will be in Auchonvillers. He explains to Gray how he knows this area. Despite being told he will be fighting mostly with new boys, with the colloquially named Kitchener's Army, Stephen tells Gray he wants to stay in the same position. Before leaving, Gray warns Stephen against revealing his superstitions to the men and wonders if Stephen's interest in this is associated with his upbringing.

CONTEXT

Kitchener's Army is the colloquial name for troops recruited for the purposes of the war. Lord Kitchener was the Secretary of State for War and his face was used on recruitment posters telling Britons 'Your Country Needs You'.

When back on the front line, Stephen takes Weir to the home of two prostitutes. Weir looks 'shaken and pale' as he returns from seeing the older prostitute (p. 203). Stephen follows the younger woman and, when he remembers Isabelle, he takes out his knife and runs the handle over her body.

On their return, the men are still preparing to move and Jack reads the letter he has received from Margaret telling him that their son has died.

Gray takes Stephen to see Colonel Barclay, the commanding officer, and, although Stephen and Gray express concern, Barclay is confident that their impending attack will be over soon despite the strong German defences.

COMMENTARY

The dehumanising influence of war and some latent misogyny is described when Stephen takes Weir to the home of the prostitutes. The **motif** of the red room resurfaces when Stephen is led into the bedroom and he is 'aghast' momentarily (p. 204). This links us and Stephen directly back to his first sexual encounters with Isabelle, and this plays a part in his recall of her.

It is telling that when Stephen remembers the last time he had sex – six years ago (with Isabelle) – his tenderness towards the prostitute dissolves: 'The body was only flesh, but she had taken hers away from him; and in her physical absence there was more than missing flesh: there was abandonment' (p. 206). He also begins to see the body of the woman he is with as 'animal matter, less dear, less valuable than the flesh of men he had seen die' (p. 206). When he takes out his knife and strokes the handle across her, we are asked to consider how the violence he has witnessed has affected him.

In the earlier parts of the novel Stephen's connection with Isabelle was one of admirer then lover, but there is the suggestion that she had fulfilled some type of maternal role, highlighted by their age difference. The parallel between his mother and lover becomes more apparent here as he feels that they both abandoned him: these two women and the prostitute momentarily **symbolise** something to despise.

CHECK THE NET

Find more details about strategy and intended outcomes of the Battle of the Somme, at **www.firstworldwar.com/battles/somme.htm**

The infamous inadequacies of the directors of the First World War, such as the British Commander-in-Chief Sir Douglas Haig, come under some scrutiny when Stephen meets Colonel Barclay. We are told that Haig is 'dead set' on having the cavalry breach the defences, and this is despite the effectiveness of enemy machine guns (p. 210). Barclay's over-confidence and terrifying lack of understanding are also mentioned. He considers Gray and Stephen to have 'faint-hearts' because of their (accurate) assessment that the Germans will have strong defences and a military advantage because they are established on the higher ground (p. 211). Barclay's arrogance is apparent; it typifies the outlook of those in power both historically and in the novel.

GLOSSARY

194 BEF British Expeditionary Force

200 CSM Command Sergeant Major

212 batman an officer's servant

PAGES 213–40

- The battalion marches to Colincamps and Stephen and his men stay in a barn.
- As Stephen's company marches to the front, they pass men digging a hole.
- The build-up for the attack, delayed for two days, is described.
- The company takes part in the first day of the Battle of the Somme.
- At the end of the day, only 155 of 800 men in the battalion respond when their names are called.

On the night the battalion reach Colincamps, the bombardment of enemy lines can be heard. The sound increases as time passes and the vibrations can be felt in the barn that Stephen and his men are using as a billet.

As Stephen marches with his company to the front, he notices a hole of thirty yards square being dug; he realises it is intended for the burial of the dead in the forthcoming attack. Before Stephen can distract them, the men notice and they move on to Auchonvillers in silence.

When they reach the village, Barclay tells the men about their impending attack; he uses patriotic rhetoric. The military police then tell the men that any who shirk their duties will be considered cowards and shot on the spot. The fear of the men is described and when the push is delayed for two days because of rain their anxieties are further heightened. Many write letters home; Stephen writes to Isabelle.

CONTEXT

On the first day of the Battle of the Somme, on 1 July 1916, there were 58,000 British casualties; a third of these lost their lives. This remains a record for the loss of life of British troops in this time frame.

The attack begins fifteen minutes after the mine in the ridge is blown. Stephen tries to follow the orders he has been given, including continuing to go forward; many men are described as they fall with their injuries. The carnage is observed by Jack and Shaw and they clutch each other in 'disbelief' (p. 229). Jack feels something die in him and Shaw weeps. The padre (military chaplain, or priest), Horrocks, pulls off his cross and throws it down (p. 230).

Among the suffering Stephen witnesses, he sees Byrne killed as he tries to get through the German wire. This wire was supposed to have been destroyed by the bombardment, but many of the shells failed to explode. Later, German snipers blow Byrne's head off his body.

Stephen leaves the shell hole he has been sheltering in when he is no longer able to stand the smell of flesh. He reaches the river and drinks from it. He loses his balance and is taken downstream and finds himself among a group of German prisoners. The British soldiers refuse to help the Germans and fire on them as Stephen is pulled out of the water. Back on the bank, Stephen's fragmented thoughts turn to Isabelle, the red room, his grandfather's cottage and the office he used to work in.

As dusk descends, he begins to walk to the German line but is injured. A tunneller, Tyson, who has been 'volunteered' to assist the wounded, applies a dressing to Stephen's leg. Stephen then takes refuge in a shell hole once more and Tyson says he will send Captain Weir over to him. The roll-call reveals that of the 800 men of their battalion who went over the top that day, only 155 answer their name.

Weir comes to Stephen and as he tells Stephen of the deaths and chaos he has seen Stephen tries to quieten him. Towards evening, the injured men come out from the shell holes they have been lying in and Weir becomes more disturbed at the sound they make. This section ends with Weir asking Stephen to hold him, and Stephen does so.

COMMENTARY

The carnage of the first day of the Somme is central to this section and is re-enacted authentically with its use of **realism** and poignancy as the **narrative** slows down time to capture the agony the men suffer as they wait to go into battle and likely death. Faulks's description of the believers and non-believers taking communion reflects this dread: 'Communion was over, but some men could not stand up again. They stayed kneeling. Having communed with their beginnings they wanted to die where they were without enduring the day ahead of them' (p. 219).

CHECK THE POEM

Siegfried Sassoon's 'Suicide in the Trenches' (1918) depicts the disastrous effects of war by focusing on one 'simple soldier boy'.

The sound of the bombardment of the enemy lines prior to the ill-fated attack emphasises the unnaturalness of the circumstances and the horror they are all involved in. It is **symbolic** that it is difficult to follow the words of Horrocks, the padre, because of this 'terrible crashing of the sky', as the tenets of Christianity are muffled by, if not completely lost to, the sound of warfare (p. 219).

The inadequacy of the orders the men are given is made obvious as they are told to walk slowly and forwards into machine-gun fire. The previous bombardment of the enemy lines was supposed to have broken enemy defences, but as they are given wire cutters it is made apparent that this is not the case. Gray explains to Stephen what a terrible error has been made by 'Haig, Rawlinson, the lot. Don't tell your men, Wraysford. Don't tell them, just pray for them' (p. 220).

The descriptions of the attack are given mainly through the perspective of Stephen as he sees men killed before they climb out of the trenches. He also sees Gray shout encouragement to the men and notices Colonel Barclay ahead of him carrying a sword. Other perspectives emphasise the disbelief in what is happening: for example, as Jack and Shaw clutch each other as they witness the men being sent into this 'hurricane' (p. 229). In addition, Horrocks's loss of faith is evident to Jack: 'His old reflex still persisting, he fell to his knees, but he did not pray. ... Jack knew what had died in him' (p. 230).

The **theme** of the war being a crime against nature is used constantly in the novel. It is perhaps at its most significant when Weir hears the sound of the injured moaning as they try to return back to their lines: 'Weir began to cry. "What have we done, what have we done? Listen to it. We've done something terrible, we'll never get back to how it was before"' (p. 239).

Furthermore, the soil is **personified** as 'groaning' and 'protesting' at this new world that has come with a rupture from past certainties (p. 239). By giving the soil human characteristics, and showing its resistance to this human catastrophe, the narrative captures how the impact of this day should and will live on. The tragedy also highlights the violent capacity of humankind and the use of personification demonstrates **figuratively** the scale of destruction. Even the earth is rebelling against this human-made apocalypse.

CONTEXT
Modernism is a movement in the arts that was greatly influenced by the destruction of certainties following the First World War. Key writers associated with the movement are Virginia Woolf, T. S. Eliot and James Joyce.

Love is also a central theme and this comes in as the men write letters home prior to the attack and at the end of the day when Weir asks Stephen to hold him. After witnessing the deaths of many and the horror of what has taken place, a gesture of love that echoes the love of a parent for a child is required by Weir. The love in the letters is similarly protective as the men try to shield their families from the worst of the atrocities; it also masks their fear, which may be interpreted as a display of bravery as well as a means to comfort those at home.

> **GLOSSARY**
>
> 213 howitzer a short cannon
> 214 timpani kettle drums
> 214 joie de vivre French term meaning 'enjoyment of life'
> 219 Communion here, the ceremony of receiving the Christian sacrament

PART THREE: ENGLAND 1978

PAGES 241–57

- It is England, 1978, and Elizabeth Benson is on an underground train as it waits in darkness.
- Elizabeth is 38, a managing director of a clothing company; she does not have children.
- She reads of the sixtieth anniversary of the Armistice and decides to find out more about her grandfather.
- Elizabeth asks her colleagues, Irene and Erich, what they know about the First World War.

QUESTION Consider the shift forward in time to Elizabeth. What effect does this have on the narrative? Does it successfully connect the past with the present, as Faulks hoped in his Introduction?

With no introduction, the narrative of Part Three shifts forward to 1978 and a new character, Elizabeth Benson, is described as she travels on the London underground. References are made to her married lover, Robert, who lives in Brussels and her mother, who lives in Twickenham. It is also explained that Elizabeth is the managing director of a clothing company. We are told that

Elizabeth does not have children and is 38 years old. Elizabeth's married friend, Lindsay, wants her to meet someone to start a relationship with, and hopes they will have children; in this section she introduces Elizabeth to a man called Stuart for this purpose.

On reading an article about the 1918 Armistice, Elizabeth is troubled and determines to know more about her maternal grandfather. She decides to read some of his papers that her mother still has. She also asks her designers, Irene and Erich, what they know about the First World War. Erich is surprised by Elizabeth's ignorance.

Commentary

Although it is not explained at this point, Elizabeth is the granddaughter of Stephen. The introduction of her character and her quest to find out more about him are used to connect the past with the late twentieth century.

Slight connections are made to Stephen by her dislike of the underground and her relief to get outside into the open. With the allusion to a 'madman' singing *It's a Long Way to Tipperary*, this is made more concrete (p. 243). It is of note that she works in clothing because Stephen also worked in the textile industry before the outbreak of war. Other and more mystical links are made as Elizabeth feels that for some unexplained reason a greater knowledge of the war will help her understand 'her own life and its choices' (p. 250). The word 'its' is used rather than 'her' and this suggests an inability on her part to take control of the choices she has made so far.

> **CONTEXT**
>
> Written in 1912, *It's a Long Way to Tipperary* is one of the most famous of the songs associated with the period of the First World War.

Faulks implies that Elizabeth's ignorance of what happened in the First World War might be something to be ashamed of. Her bid to discover more is instigated by the anniversary of the Armistice and by thoughts of her grandfather, but she is also the means to demonstrate that this shared history should always be remembered. This point is emphasised in the way the narrative is constructed, with this section coming immediately after the description of the events of the first day of the Battle of the Somme.

This section also draws on the subject of childlessness and may be seen as introducing the concept that having children is expected and even vital. Her age is referred to in negative terms: she is coming closer to the age of the menopause and her time is running out to have children. These points are left unchallenged in the narrative, which seems to communicate the message that it is natural for women to want to have children.

QUESTION
This novel stresses the importance of childbirth – by subscribing to this ethos, can Elizabeth still be viewed as a feminist character?

GLOSSARY

247 couture designer clothing or high fashion

251 navvy an informal term for a labourer; a corruption of 'navigator', which referred to the labourers on canals

---

PAGES 258–78

- On her way to France, Elizabeth looks at a book about the First World War.
- In France, she visits the Thiepval memorial.
- Elizabeth goes on to Belgium to see Robert.
- When back in England, she visits her mother. Her connection to Stephen is revealed.
- Elizabeth takes Stephen's notebook to Bob and he offers to decode it.
- Elizabeth goes on a date with Stuart – she enjoys his company but her thoughts turn to Robert.

On the cross-channel ferry to France, Elizabeth looks at the history book lent to her by Irene's partner, Bob; she is particularly struck by the photographs in it. She is on her way to see Robert in Belgium and has decided to stop off in northern France first. She goes to the Thiepval memorial and is overcome by the lists of names of British men who went missing or were presumed dead in the First World War.

In Brussels, Elizabeth stays with Robert. Before she leaves she asks when they will marry. He says this will happen within three years, but she says that she thinks this is too late and on being prompted she admits that she would like to have children. Robert is married and says it is not possible to divorce yet. He tells her she is free to find somebody else, but she says she loves him.

After Elizabeth returns to England, she looks in her mother's attic for information regarding her grandfather. She sees items belonging to her father that were from the Second World War and then moves on to discover a military handbook and a coded notebook that were Stephen's. The military handbook is inscribed 'Captain Stephen Wraysford, April 1917'. She puts the notebook in her pocket and takes it with her.

When she comes downstairs, she discusses her grandfather with her mother, and her mother says how she wishes Elizabeth had known him. On the following Saturday, Elizabeth shows the notebook to Bob and he says how although it is written in Greek script, Greek words are not used; he offers to decode the notebook for her.

Stuart asks Elizabeth out for dinner. Afterwards they go back to his flat and he plays the piano. Elizabeth enjoys the evening, but she realises she will never leave Robert, because he doesn't 'threaten her independence' (p. 278).

COMMENTARY

The past is connected to the present through Elizabeth's growing interest in Stephen. Her search for more information is driven by her lack of knowledge of history and by her view that an understanding of the past will enable her to know more about herself. When she sees the Thiepval memorial, she says 'Nobody told me', a reaction possibly demonstrating the necessity of knowing about this massive loss of life (p. 264). Elizabeth may be interpreted as a cipher for highlighting how easy it is for information to be lost in a relatively short time-frame.

Elizabeth's childlessness is seen to preoccupy her and is even a part of her inspiration to find out more about her heritage, even though this is set out in negative terms: 'If she had no children herself she should at least understand what had gone before her; she ought to know what line she was not continuing' (p. 261). Thoughts of the next generation are also used to connect to the possibilities of other

CHECK THE NET

The huge Thiepval memorial lists the names of over 70,000 soldiers who went missing during the Battle of the Somme. See the Commonwealth War Graves Commission site at **www.cwgc.org** for photographs of this monument. Click on 'Search our records' and enter 'Thiepval' into the 'Cemeteries' search box.

wars as she thinks how if she had a son there would be no guarantee he would not have to fight 'in this hellish perversion' (p. 270).

The bonds between past and present generations are discussed as Elizabeth looks through the papers in her mother's attic. There are details concerning the buying of the house and Elizabeth regards this as an effort by her mother 'to improve upon the past' because it demonstrates a parent's wish to improve the life of their child in the form of sacrifice (p. 271). This leads her to think momentarily about whether she is deserving of this: 'Yet still somehow it was difficult to see her own life as the pinnacle of previous generations' sacrifices' (p. 271). This refers not only to her mother's love, but also to the sacrifices of those who have fought in wars.

The discovery of the military handbook and notebook reintroduces Stephen fully to us and solves the mystery about the identity of Elizabeth's grandfather. Clues are also given that tell of Stephen's fate after the Somme. His military handbook, which instructs the officers to be 'blood thirsty', reveals that he was promoted to Captain and tells us that he survived at least until April 1917 (p. 271). Further to this, Elizabeth's mother remembers him and we therefore learn that he survived the war.

The directive to be 'blood thirsty' rather than bloodthirsty has an effect on Elizabeth when she reads it: 'Something about the way the word "bloodthirsty" was split in two made Elizabeth shudder' (p. 271). Her squeamishness is understandable to modern readers and, compared with the experiences Stephen underwent, it highlights her relatively secure existence.

CHECK THE POEM

Compare Elizabeth with the eponymous heroine in 'Miss Gee' (1937) by W. H. Auden and consider how both characters are used to question the 'normality' of the woman who does not want children.

GLOSSARY

260 **seraglio** the quarters used by women in a Muslim house or palace

264 **Albert Speer** architect who worked for the Nazi regime in the 1930s and 1940s

271 **fissile** possible to split easily

275 **Linear B** an ancient script used between 1500 BC and 1200 BC in the areas of Crete and the southern Greece mainland

PART FOUR: FRANCE 1917

PAGES 279–98

- It is now 1917 and Stephen and his men are marching to the front line.
- Stephen has taken over the company from Gray, who is now the battalion commander.
- When on home leave, Weir realises his parents have no understanding of the conditions he has endured.
- Stephen reads Weir's fortune.
- Stephen tries to explain the beliefs he has had since being badly injured and Jack writes home to his wife.

It has been raining for three weeks and as Stephen and the men march to the front line they are able to smell the latrines and the dead bodies that are decomposing. Only three of the men – Stephen, Petrossian and Brennan – are from the original platoon. At times Stephen feels real affection for the men, his curiosity about finding the limits of what they will endure has eased off because he knows there are none. Ellis, who now shares the dugout with Stephen, thinks Weir is too old to be doing the job he does and is disturbed by his appearance.

On Weir's visit to his parents, he discovers difficulties in explaining to them the conditions he has suffered. His parents barely refer to the war and although Weir expects to feel at home after a while, this does not happen. The house and the views from it are familiar but he has no 'sense of belonging' (p. 287). He tries to tell his father how terrible the war is, but is unable to articulate his feelings and asks for a drink instead.

Back in Stephen's dugout, Weir asks him to read his fortune and after following a ritual involving a dead rat and laying out cards Stephen tells him it is good. Weir is pleased, but says he knows the pack of cards was fixed and Stephen denies this.

The conversation turns to magic and then religion. Stephen tries to explain the faith he has had since being badly injured. When

CHECK THE BOOK

Andrea Levy's *Small Island* (2004) is a novel concerned with the Second World War. Its central **theme** is the part played by the non-Britons who fought for the colonialist power.

Ellis questions if this is Christianity, Stephen feels the rage he felt as a child and then controls himself.

The section ends with Jack and his letter to Margaret. He says how they are doing and refers to the padre's lecture on the Prodigal Son.

COMMENTARY

In Part Four, the **narrative** has moved forward to France in 1917 and there are references to the changes in the men that have been brought about by the effects of the war. The contrast between their previous lives and how the conditions have altered their opinions and relationships is conveyed through Faulks's description of Weir's visit home to his parents. He hopes for the 'familiar wash of normality' when he takes a bath, but finds this does not happen (p. 287). In this paragraph, the word 'familiar' is used three times to emphasise how unfamiliar everything feels, and how different this is to what he expected. His old clothes no longer fit him and even the 'familiar view' from the window gives him no sense of belonging. It seems that the war has altered him irrevocably.

The conversation between Weir and his father is stilted. Weir's broken speech, which is filled with pauses and failed attempts to explain what he has suffered, conveys how difficult it is to put these unheard-of experiences into words (p. 289). His parents' reluctance to understand is a reminder of the soldiers' alienation from their former lives.

The war has placed a barrier between Weir and his family. This is voiced when Weir says in the dugout that his father was 'bored' when he tried to tell him about his experiences. He wishes 'a great bombardment' would smash Piccadilly and Whitehall 'and kill the whole lot of them' (p. 294). After being prompted about his family, he says 'particularly them' (p. 294).

With the introduction of the new character Ellis, the changes in the men are made more evident. We are able to see how Weir appears to be bitter, strange and frightening to this naive young man who has had little experience of the war. When he notices how much Weir's hands shake we do too. Conversely, Ellis's innocence is

> **CONTEXT**
>
> The parable of the Prodigal Son is taken from the New Testament, from Luke 15.11–32. It tells of the son who asks for his share of his father's inheritance while the father is still alive and returns home after wasting it. His father accepts him back and celebrates with a 'fatted calf'.

revealed when he says how he wants to win the war and Weir looks at him with incredulity (p. 293).

Such increasing disillusion is also depicted in Stephen's waning curiosity about the limits the men will go to because he now knows 'there were no boundaries they would not cross, no limits to what they would endure' (p. 282). He also knows that although they look 'passive', 'they had locked up in their hearts the horror of what they had seen, and their jovial pride in their resilience was not convincing' (p.282)

The **theme** of fathers and lost sons is used when Weir returns home, and also when, in a letter, Jack tells Margaret about the sermon of the Prodigal Son. His spirituality and feelings for his own son are expressed when he says how he would have done his best for their John. This parable may be read in comparison to the reception Weir receives from his parents on his home leave. For him and the other lost sons of his generation, there is no 'fatted calf', only politeness and lack of understanding or empathy for what he may have endured.

Spirituality, or a sense of faith, is **alluded** to when Stephen mentions his altered perspective since being badly injured. The closeness to death has shown him something beyond himself: he attempts to articulate it as '[a] room, a place, some self-grounded place' (p. 296). Although traditional beliefs in Christianity appear to be shattered, as shown by the **metaphor** of the Prodigal Son, and when the padre throws down his cross (p. 230), Stephen becomes the vehicle for discussing a faith that is not contained by institutions.

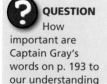

QUESTION
How important are Captain Gray's words on p. 193 to our understanding of Stephen's character?

Stephen also reveals that as a child he used to believe in magic power. He says this was because, 'I wanted to have a make-believe world because I couldn't bear to live in the real one' (p. 295). It is also suggested that this desire for a 'make-believe world' that unhappy children experience may equally be applied to men such as Stephen who are searching for something to make good the evil that is occurring around them. Stephen may be disillusioned with organised religion, but his turn to superstition and the view that there is something beyond human existence exemplifies the make-believe world that comforted Stephen as a child.

GLOSSARY

291 obsequious   overly attentive, deferential

PAGES 299–323

- Stephen follows Weir down into the tunnels.
- A canary escapes in the tunnel and despite Stephen's phobia of birds he has to bring it back to the exit shaft.
- Stephen joins Ellis on a trip to Amiens.
- While there, Stephen sees a woman in a bar and realises she must be Isabelle's sister, Jeanne, and they talk.
- Jeanne gives him some information about what has happened to Isabelle.

CONTEXT

Canaries were used in tunnels and mines as a means of checking for gas. The death of the canary signified that the air was poisoned.

Weir convinces Stephen to come down in the tunnels after an explosion has killed two of their men, Shaw and Stanley, at a listening post. Weir takes a canary with him, and Stephen crawls after him. When they reach the earth where the men are trapped, Weir discovers they cannot be dug out because this will bring down the roof. Timbers are needed to support it. All they can do for the men now is say a prayer for them. Stephen says the prayer and they turn to go back.

Weir's pick accidentally catches on the roof of the tunnel. This brings down clay and Weir's arm is broken. Stephen lifts the clay off him, and Weir tells Stephen to take the canary. However, the cage has been broken in the fall of earth and it has escaped. It is a court-martial offence to leave a canary in the tunnel so Stephen has to catch it. Stephen screams and shakes when the bird brushes against him, but Weir catches it and gives it to him. Stephen makes a sling for it and carries it in his mouth as he crawls along; he is relieved once they come back up to the trenches.

Ellis and Stephen are given leave to go to Amiens; on the way Stephen admits to fixing the cards to give Weir a good reading.

In Amiens, changes have been made since the bombardments and occupation. Stephen eventually finds a bar where locals still drink

CHECK THE BOOK

The Monocled Mutineer (1979) by William Allison and John Fairley was adapted for television in 1986 by Alan Bleasdale. It tells of a mutiny by British soldiers in the First World War.

and here he encounters Jeanne. He tells her about his time with Isabelle and she warily informs him of Isabelle's movements since he last saw her. They arrange to meet the next day so she can let him know if Isabelle will see him again.

COMMENTARY

The motif of birds as a symbol of fear as well as innocence is used here as Stephen is forced to take the canary after Weir breaks his arm. It is telling that despite Stephen's phobia and the experiences both have gone through, neither man is able to kill the canary and instead choose to bring it safely back with them. Stephen imagines a fossil, of 'a pterodactyl ribbed in limestone' (p. 306). The simile is carried over in to page 324 when he thinks of Isabelle as a 'fossil memory' that has come to life since his return to Amiens. The use of the fossil denotes a longstanding memory that has been preserved and, in the case of his fear of birds, it has been with him for as long as he can remember.

The trip to Amiens is also an excursion into the past. The changes that have occurred there reveal an outcome of the war that differs from the front-line experience. Stephen is told how the town was occupied by the Germans in 1914 and 'stupid ones' and 'cowards' were rounded up as '[t]he rest made their own arrangements' (p. 312). He also discovers that the Azaire home has been damaged and notices how many of the women in the street are wearing black.

The encounter with Jeanne re-introduces the theme of love and moves the narrative away from the main focus of the war. The memory of Isabelle has been resurrected by the visit to Amiens and Stephen's conversation with her sister. In addition, a connection is made with the earlier part of the novel set in 1910 and so the narrative is held together. The details that Lisette is to marry and Grégoire is to join the army next year mark the passing of time and remind us how the next generation may also be caught up in the war.

GLOSSARY

308 **Thucydides** an historian of Ancient Greece, author of the *History of the Peloponnesian War*

320 **exculpate** clear from guilt

PAGES 324–41

- Jeanne tells Stephen that Isabelle has agreed to see him.
- Stephen visits Isabelle.
- She does not tell him they have a daughter, but informs him of the Prussian officer she has grown to love.
- On his return, Gray tells Stephen that he must take promotion and home leave now.
- They discuss the killing of prisoners-of-war and Stephen says that dignity is required for the future.

Stephen walks to the old Azaire home and is overcome with memories. He walks all night and meets Jeanne in the bar as they arranged. She tells him that Isabelle has agreed to see him and he is invited to come to her home that evening. When Stephen visits Isabelle, the room is darkened but he notices her face is now disfigured and she holds herself differently since being injured by an exploding shell. He controls his rage and she explains that she returned to Amiens and Azaire because of her father's machinations and the pleading of Azaire's children.

Isabelle explains that the Germans occupied the town and demanded provisions; hostages were required to make sure the German demands were met. As a member of the council, Azaire volunteered to be a hostage and he also saw it as his duty to report for deportation. She does not tell Stephen of the daughter she has had (and that he is the father) but does let him know about the Prussian officer, Max, whom she has grown to love and has stayed in touch with since he left the area.

Stephen hears a sound, which he thinks is a child, but Isabelle tells him it is cats. He touches Isabelle's face gently, tracing her scar. She becomes aroused, and when he leaves she covers her face with her hands.

When Stephen reports to Gray, he is told that he must accept promotion and home leave now. Stephen agrees only reluctantly after being reminded of how his knowledge of French is of use to

 CHECK THE BOOK

Scars Upon My Heart (1981), edited by Catherine Reilly, is a collection of poems by women from the First World War. The title is taken from a poem written by Vera Brittain for her brother. The collection includes work by Rose Macauley, Nancy Cunard and Charlotte Mew. It highlights the impact the war had on those not actually on the front line.

the army. They then discuss the shooting of enemy prisoners. Stephen says that he prefers to go by the rule book and that he also knows the necessity of keeping some dignity. He reminds Gray that on the first day of the Battle of the Somme he saw 'perfect blankness' in Gray's eyes, and adds that both have seen the 'great void' in each other's soul (p. 341).

COMMENTARY

The theme of love is drawn upon in this section when Isabelle relates to Stephen how she has grown to love Max. The difficulties in their coming together have made them more determined: 'The more difficult it became, the more important they both knew that it was for them to honour the pledges they had made to each other' (p. 334). As is typical of romantic lovers in literature, the obstacles to their love are seen to bring them together as separation heightens the appeal of the romance.

Isabelle's relationship with Max contradicts our expectations because it may have seemed posssible that Isabelle and Stephen would be reconciled at this point. However, this lack of unity is in keeping with the themes of loss and the fracture of certainties, which are central to this war story. Furthermore, this allows the knowledge of Stephen's daughter to be held back to maintain the tension.

QUESTION Consider the change in Azaire's character. Does this sense of responsibility to the town sit well with Faulks's earlier depiction of him as a violent misogynist?

Isabelle's details about Azaire and his more recent conduct serve to rehabilitate his character. He is depicted as monstrous if fragile earlier in the novel, but since the war and the German occupation of Amiens he is given heroic status because he volunteers to be a hostage and then to be deported. This change may be interpreted as exemplifying the possibilities that war gives to show heroism.

The challenge to nihilism comes here and elsewhere in the guise of discussing the future generations. When Stephen says that prisoners-of-war should not be killed, for example, he argues: 'It sounds strange, but we have degraded human life so far that we must leave some space for dignity to grow again. As it may, one day. Not for you or me, but for our children' (p. 340). This desire to preserve a sense of humanity is not for this generation that has been afflicted by what they have seen and done, because as Stephen points out they may be damaged beyond repair: 'I saw the great void in your soul, and you saw mine' (p. 341). However, the consideration for those who come after them allows for the possibility of a return to relative normalcy.

The reference to the next generation is an example of **dramatic irony** because Stephen is unaware at this point that he has a daughter. This has the effect of making his argument for dignity all the more poignant because he does not realise that he is speaking literally rather than **metaphorically**.

PAGES 342–64

- After burying Shaw, Jack is overcome with grief when he performs his comedy routine at a local estaminet, or café.
- Jeanne writes to Stephen and tells him that Isabelle has gone to Munich to be with Max.
- Ellis, Stephen, Weir, Jack and Brennan are part of a working party that retrieves the dead from no-man's-land.
- Stephen's goes back to England for his leave and feels a delayed sense of shock.

Jack attends the burial of Shaw and Stanley, and goes to an estaminet with Evans and Jones to toast Shaw's life. They sing and Jack performs his music-hall routine, but breaks down gradually with grief and chokes as he tries to sing.

Jeanne writes to Stephen and lets him know that Isabelle has gone to Munich to be with Max; he finds he is now able to bear this news. He remembers the time in the cathedral in 1910 when he foresaw the numbers of dead, and connects this with his love for Isabelle.

A working party is formed to collect the dead from no-man's-land and they see many decomposing corpses. Brennan finds his dead brother and brings him back for burial. He tells Stephen that he thinks of himself as lucky because he missed the first day of the Battle of the Somme and has now found his brother. Brennan sings in memory of his brother all night.

CHECK THE BOOK

Men Who March Away (1965) is a collection of war poems edited by Ian Parsons. It takes its title from the Thomas Hardy poem, which focuses on soldiers marching to the front.

Before going on leave to England, Stephen stays in Boulogne, in a hotel with other officers who have been on the front for only six months. He writes to Jeanne about how important his friendship with her is to him. He then tears it up because of the informal tone and writes another instead, including 'some details of his train journey to Boulogne', and promising that he would write from England 'when at least he would have something interesting to tell her' (p. 354).

In England, Stephen feels isolated because of his experiences. He notices that the war does not make headline news any more. He travels to Norfolk, because Weir once told him how pleasant it is, and begins to feel the aftershock of being on the front line. When he goes for a walk, he has a moment of profound revelation, as he feels a sense of forgiveness and a love for nature.

COMMENTARY

The camaraderie and love between the men on the front line is demonstrated through Jack's grief for Shaw. The cramped living conditions have forced them to be physically close, which has given him comfort previously. His mourning becomes apparent to others when he breaks down while performing for the men at the estaminet. He falters when he begins to sing *If You Were the Only Girl in the World* and thinks how Shaw had been 'in this strange alternate life, the only person in the world to him' (p. 345). It is not stated outright that theirs was a homosexual relationship, but it is evident that Jack's grief is bound up in love and may be described as homosocial: a platonic love between men. However, if one bears in mind the song that chokes him, there are suggestions that Jack's love in this 'alternate life' may have had a homosexual element.

> **CONTEXT**
>
> Homosexuality was illegal in the British Armed Forces until 2000.

Graphic depictions of decomposed bodies are given when the men join the working party to retrieve the dead. A rat emerges from the abdomen of a corpse and Stephen thinks the dead are no longer men but 'flesh and flies' (p. 351). The brutality is heightened when Brennan finds the torso of his brother's corpse and carries it back for burial. When he tells Stephen that he feels 'lucky' for having missed the carnage of the Somme, and for finding his brother, the poignancy of the situation is heightened (p. 352).

What seems like the inevitable continuity of the soldiers' experience of war is highlighted when Stephen comes across some young officers in Boulogne: 'They had not been there for the great slaughters of the previous year and could not see the mechanized abattoir that was expected in the impassable mud of Flanders in the months to come' (p. 353).

The third-person **narrator** signals that unknown to them they are now in the 'entr'acte' (p. 353). This term refers to an interlude or performance between two acts of a play: its usage suggests that war is being compared to a theatrical event (as in the theatre of war) and that they are all playing their assigned roles in the drama.

The developing relationship between Stephen and Jeanne is mentioned when he writes to her from Boulogne. He thinks of her features and compares them to Isabelle's, and knows that he needs to be formal with her 'for the time being' (p. 354). He does not want to be 'precipitate and vulgar' with her, but he also wants to say how much he values her friendship (p. 354). The distance he maintains is in accord with the greater formality of the time, especially when compared to the 1970s when Elizabeth appears; it also emphasises his wariness of becoming attached to another at this time of crisis.

The soldier's isolation, which has come about with the knowledge he has gained on the front line, is examined on Stephen's return to England. The faces of the crowd show their shock at the sight of these men who do not fit the propagandist's image of the all-conquering heroes. The war no longer makes headline news and Stephen is treated disrespectfully in a shop. He recognises how the war is now increasingly overlooked: 'He would have been embarrassed to be treated differently from ordinary civilians ... but it seemed strange to him that his presence was a matter not just of indifference but resentment' (p. 358). These details emphasise both his loneliness and the ignorance of those whom the troops are told they are fighting for.

The **motif** of the Prodigal Son is used once more when Stephen experiences his 'binding love' for nature and a sense of affinity with the world around him. He thinks of Isabelle, his mother and Weir

CHECK THE BOOK
Compare the epiphany experienced by Stephen to that by Gabriel Conroy in 'The Dead', which is the final story in James Joyce's *The Dubliners* (1914).

and how 'nothing was immoral or beyond redemption' (p. 363). The parable is used at this point to express his forgiveness for what has happened to him and those he loves (before and during the war); Stephen's emotion is comparable to that which the father of the story feels for his lost son.

PAGES 365–90

- Stephen visits Jeanne.
- Back on the front, Gray tells Stephen they are preparing for another attack.
- Stephen survives the attack.
- Weir is killed by a sniper's bullet.
- Stephen visits Jeanne again.

On his return to France, Stephen visits Jeanne and when the time comes to leave he dreads going back to war because of the effort required. The situation reminds him of when he was a child and how much he hated being taken from the fields to return to the institution.

 CHECK THE POEM

Siegfried Sassoon's 'The Dug-Out' (1919) is a moving poem about a premonition of the death of a friend in the First World War.

Back on the front, Stephen is told of the imminent attack on the enemy and how he must lead his men towards the canal. The night before the attack, Weir tries to tell Stephen of a premonition he has had and that he wants to say goodbye to him. Stephen refuses to listen and throws him out of the dugout and on to the floor of the trench. When alone, Stephen thinks of his mother and how he does not want to die.

This time, the attack is described as being better conceived than that on the first day of the Battle of the Somme because they are told to run instead of march slowly. Stephen is among some men who make advances, but they are finally ordered to withdraw because of bad communication between those who are giving the orders. Ellis is killed and Stephen knows he will have to write to his mother to inform her of this.

Before the attack on the Messines Ridge, the mines are set underground. Weir is then shot by a sniper when he stands on an unprotected part of the parapet. Stephen grieves and Gray comes to talk to him. Gray explains that because of Stephen's knowledge of French they need his help to talk to the French allies because there are rumours of a mutiny; Stephen thus takes part in an intelligence-gathering operation.

Stephen visits Jeanne in August and September and she tells him to be strong for her sake. He says that he feels guilty for surviving when others have been killed, and he is now barely managing to exist.

COMMENTARY

Loving and grieving are used as central themes here. Stephen recognises that his new-found affinity with the world makes the thought of entering into another attack impossible: 'His renewed love of the world made the prospect of leaving it unbearable' (pp. 374–5).

Stephen's love for Weir and consequent grief when he is killed are of great importance in this section. His feelings of loss are described as a form of 'listlessness' (p. 390) and his love for the world continues but 'he feared that the reality he now inhabited was very fragile' (p. 388). The numbness that Jeanne spots in him drives her to urge him to 'be strong for my sake' (p. 390); she reminds him there is a God. Stephen's increased isolation following the death of Weir is both understandable and moving: 'His life became grey and thin, like a light that might at any moment be extinguished; it was filled with quietness' (p. 390). The physical and mental danger he is in is exemplified by the ephemeral quality of the light his life is compared to.

 CHECK THE NET

The Channel 4 website has a micro site that gives information about the First World War, including biographies of key politicians and military figures and a timeline from 1914 to 1918. Go to **www.channel4.com** and type 'First World War' into the search box. On the First World War homepage, select 'Overview' and click on '1917' for information about disaffection and threats of mutiny.

GLOSSARY

376 **Mills bombs** forms of grenade

388 **MC** Military Cross

PART FIVE: ENGLAND 1978–79

PAGES 391–422

- Bob has still not solved the code used in Stephen's notebook.
- Elizabeth locates a now elderly Colonel Gray.
- With the information she receives from Gray's wife, Elizabeth visits Brennan who is in a nursing home.
- Elizabeth learns she is pregnant.
- Bob gives Elizabeth the translation of the notebook after finally solving the code.

Part Five returns to England in 1978 and at this point Bob has still not made progress in solving the code of Stephen's notebook. Elizabeth follows up information she has about Stephen and finds a number to contact Gray (who is referred to as Colonel Gray). As they talk, he remembers more about Stephen; his wife says Elizabeth should get in touch with Brennan who is in a Star and Garter home in Southend.

CONTEXT

Founded in 1916, the Royal Star and Garter homes give care to disabled ex-servicemen and women.

On visiting Brennan, Elizabeth discovers how his leg was amputated in October 1918 and that he suffered shell-shock. He has lived there permanently since 1923 and his last visitor came in 1949. Brennan is one of many residents who have no interest in the world outside. As they talk, his confusion is revealed, but Elizabeth thinks that a connection with the past has been made for her.

Elizabeth's mother has found twenty more of Stephen's notebooks. Later, Stuart, who is the man she met at the home of her friend Lindsay, calls to see Elizabeth. She is shocked when he unexpectedly asks her to marry him.

In January, Elizabeth decides to visit Brennan again. When she returns home she takes a pregnancy test and discovers that she is pregnant. The next day, Bob contacts her to let her know that he has solved the code, and he posts her some of the translation.

COMMENTARY

The connection between the past and the present of the late 1970s is made again with the shift to Elizabeth. This link is established more firmly when she contacts both Gray and Brennan in the hope of discovering more information about Stephen. These sections are framed with references to his notebooks, which also connect his and Elizabeth's lives. The presence of these notebooks in the 1970s emphasises the significance history has within this narrative. Bob's translation reveals that Stephen wrote, 'No child or future generation will ever know what this was like. They will never understand' (p. 422). Elizabeth is portrayed as someone who refuses to sever herself from the past any longer and this has the effect of alleviating the despondent tone set by Stephen's narrative.

Comparisons between the past and present as well as connections are also made here. This is most telling when Elizabeth considers her life to be 'frivolous' (p. 413) in relation to what people endured during the First World War: 'She thought of Tom Brennan, who had known only life or death, then death in life. In her generation there was no intensity' (p. 414). This lack of intensity may be viewed as a pleasurable result of not having to fight in a war, but the comparably 'frivolous' life she leads is a counterbalance to the suffering her grandfather and men like him were exposed to. It demonstrates, by comparison, how great his privations were.

Brennan is used as a living reminder of the horrors that war can inflict on the living. He is unable to distinguish between the past and present and confuses events of different years as he conflates the Boer War with the First and Second World Wars. It is as though he has retreated from the reality he has known in the war and, as the nurse tells Elizabeth of the residents of the nursing home, 'This is all they know, all they remember' (p. 400).

Brennan is a **symbol** for remembering those who served in the war. He is also a **trope** for pointing out the significance of history – a reminder that the past should not be forgotten. Before leaving him after her first visit, Elizabeth reflects on how 'she had somehow kept the chain of experience intact' (p. 404). On her visit to him in January she promises she will keep in contact with him or another

CHECK THE BOOK

Shell-shock was recognised as a form of what is now known as post-traumatic stress disorder by psychoanalysts such as Sigmund Freud. Pat Barker's *Regeneration* trilogy (1991–5) draws on it as a central theme.

QUESTION
Compare the use of language in the sections concerning Elizabeth with those set in the First World War. How is the 'lack of intensity' created?

of his generation as a form of repaying a debt: 'Somehow she would repay the debt; she would complete the circle' (p. 417).

As well as honouring the past, regeneration is another key theme. Elizabeth's pregnancy is used as a **symbol** to maintain the connections between the generations as the future continues in a physical form. This is elaborated on in Part Seven.

PART SIX: FRANCE 1918

PAGES 423–34

- It is now 1918 in France. Gray engages Stephen in a discussion about the regiment's memorial.
- Jack writes to Margaret and tells her that the war will move more quickly now.
- Stephen visits Jeanne before rejoining his company.
- Bérard has told Isabelle's parents that she is in Germany.
- Stephen puts his arms around Jeanne and says Isabelle's name.

Part Six is set in France, 1918. Stephen goes to see Gray, who talks about a memorial for the regiment and asks Stephen which words he would like to see used. Stephen says he does not know because he has no pride in what they have done. He is then informed that his staff attachment is over and he is to return to the front. He is indifferent to this news.

Jack writes a letter to Margaret and explains that they are now doing road work after the explosion of the Messines Ridge. He also tells her the war should go faster now and he hopes their work as tunnellers is done.

Before going back to the front, Stephen visits Jeanne in Rouen. She explains that Amiens was bombarded in the spring offensive and that is why she has returned to Rouen. She also tells him that Bérard has informed her parents about Isabelle's whereabouts and that he offered the German commandant his house when the Germans first occupied Amiens.

CHECK THE NET
There is more information about the Messines Ridge, at **www.spartacus. schoolnet.co.uk/ FWW.htm**, under 'Battles'.

Jeanne tells Stephen not to give up and says the war is nearly over. She also says she loves him and he promises to try to keep going. Later, Stephen enters Jeanne's room by mistake and turns when he sees she is naked. She tells him to come back in and when he kneels and puts his arms round her thighs he calls her Isabelle.

COMMENTARY

Stephen's despondency is a prevailing element in this section; it highlights how long the war has been going on. Both Gray and Jeanne separately try to pull him out of his inertia to remind him that it is worth continuing.

Gray attempts to encourage Stephen by asking him about the wording he would use on the regiment's memorial, but Stephen's response signifies his complete indifference and shame at what they have all done. Gray pushes him further and explains his own position too: 'Think of the words on that memorial, Wraysford. Think of those stinking towns and foul … villages whose names will be turned into some bogus glory by … historians who have sat in London. We were there. As our punishment for God knows what, we were there, and our men died in each of those disgusting places' (p. 427). He goes on to stress that the words 'Final advance and pursuit' should make people remember and bow their heads 'just a little' (p. 427). This perspective is a reminder of how the historians who were not present will have the power to rewrite history. We and Stephen are being told to consider those who are dead rather than the outcome of winners and losers.

Jeanne tries to use hope as a means to rouse Stephen from his sense of defeat and tells him that '[n]othing is beyond redemption' (p. 431). This echoes Stephen's sentiment when he experienced the 'binding love' on his walk in Norfolk in Part Four (p. 363). The language Jeanne uses has a Christian overtone and is a sign of the possibilities of forgiveness and continuance.

The pain of what has happened in the past is stifling Stephen despite the efforts of Gray and Jeanne. This is apparent when he holds Jeanne and then sobs as he says Isabelle's name. The ghosts of the

CHECK THE BOOK
The Return of the Soldier (1918) by Rebecca West has a victim of shell-shock at the centre of its **narrative**.

past keep resurfacing and the present, therefore, becomes submerged. The future is considered only with the prompting of others.

> ### GLOSSARY
> **428 RE field companies**   Royal Engineers field companies

Pages 435–54

- Weir's replacement, Cartwright, wants Stephen to go down in the tunnels.
- Although afraid, he agrees. He is terrified of the thought of not being able to turn around.
- There is an explosion and Stephen hears the sound of men dying.
- Stephen digs his way back to Jack who is badly injured.
- Stephen tells Jack he will have children for him.

Stephen reluctantly agrees to go down into the tunnels with Cartwright, Weir's replacement. Jack is told to bring Stephen back once he has finished down there and Stephen remembers the first time he went down to protect Jack. He does not know if he will be able to stay calm this time.

There is an explosion and Stephen's arm is damaged. He hears a sound and knows there is another survivor with him. After an hour of moving the soil from the man he finds it is Jack. Jack's legs are crushed and he thinks his ribs are broken. Stephen offers to carry him once he is freed and Jack tells him which way to go. Before they move on, Stephen decides to search for other survivors.

Stephen carries Jack as he would a child. At the end of this section of the tunnel they find a wall of soil from a second explosion. Stephen considers shooting himself rather than dying of thirst and starvation.

The two men talk, and Jack tells him about John. Stephen says he will have more children for him. Jack becomes more resigned to dying and Stephen becomes more determined to find a way out.

CHECK THE BOOK
Tommy (2005) by Richard Holmes uses archival material to memorialise the men who served on the British front line.

COMMENTARY

The camaraderie between the men on the front line has been a fundamental concern of the novel and is epitomised in the last section of Part Six with the forming of a friendship between Jack and Stephen. As Jack states, 'it is right that he should be rescued by someone he had himself saved; he felt confident that Stephen would deliver him' (p. 444). As well as exemplifying camaraderie, this gives the narrative a form of symmetry because Jack has previously saved Stephen and both have been asked to protect the other at different times. With the use of words such as 'saved' and 'delivered' the chance of being saved is compared to that of a biblical miracle. Stephen is given an almost God-like power through these religious implications.

Although Jack's confidence in being rescued is finally seen to be misplaced, the bond between the two men demonstrates a form of heroism in that both have shown a desire to save others. This depiction of heroism may be interpreted as a form of tribute to those who fought in this war. Faulks continues the tribute in the descriptions of Stephen's attempts to find other survivors: 'If by searching he brought death closer, it would not matter; there would be some decorum in their dying deep beneath the country they had fought so long to protect' (p. 449). By wanting to have 'decorum' and fairness, Stephen is characterised as unselfish. This counters the despair that had earlier threatened to engulf him.

The recurring themes of regeneration and having children are also drawn upon. This comes at the point when Stephen says he will have children for Jack because it is no longer possible for Jack and Margaret to do so. Jack talks about his love for John and he reveals his grief: 'In the darkness of the tunnel Jack's voice came up unexpectedly in the lament he had denied himself at the time of John's death; so close to his own time of dying, he was freed from restraint' (p. 451). Stephen says he talks as though he had fallen in love with his son, and Jack agrees. Jack also describes how his love for John was transformative: 'I wondered what my life had been about until he came along. It was nothing' (pp. 451–2). This echoes Elizabeth's sentiments about her desire to have children and is another example of how the past is connected to the present in this novel.

CHECK THE BOOK

The First Casualty (2005) by Ben Elton examines how truth becomes distorted in war. It is another novel that looks back to the First World War and the destruction of a generation.

PAGES 455–85

- Jack calls for his mother as the fear of dying takes hold of him.
- Stephen finds a stack of explosives and Jack tells him how to blow the charges.
- After three days' work Stephen creates an explosion heard on the German line.
- Lieutenant Levi and two other German soldiers, Lamm and Kroger, go to look for survivors.
- Jack dies and Stephen knocks his knife against the wall to let the search party know he has heard them.
- Stephen is rescued and he and Levi embrace.

Jack feels a hand brush against his face as they go through the tunnel and he recognises a trousered leg as belonging to Evans. He begins to lose his composure as he imagines the place being peopled by ghosts. Jack makes a sound and Stephen recognises it as the one he made when he was badly injured and was calling for his mother.

Stephen finds a stack of sandbags and explosives. It takes him three days to clear the chamber to blow it with just enough explosives to clear the way for them. Jack tells him how to set a fuse. Stephen follows the instructions and shortens the fuse to give them both distance from the explosion and lights it.

The blast is felt on the German line and Lieutenant Levi goes down with Lamm and Kroger to investigate. Levi does so in the knowledge there is a likely chance that his brother Joseph has been killed. Lamm sets off a small charge to blow the mass in front of them to clear the way.

Stephen and Jack survive the explosion Stephen set, but because it does not have the hoped-for effect, they remain trapped. Stephen considers killing himself with his knife because he has now lost his gun. The beat of his pulse deters him and he turns to talking to Jack about why he must stay alive.

CHECK THE BOOK

All Quiet on the Western Front (1929) by Erich Maria Remarque is written from the perspective of the German front line.

Lamm finds Joseph's corpse and Levi goes into mourning. He insists they continue searching for their comrades so they can be returned home; Lamm and Kroger accept his orders.

Stephen guesses he and Jack have been underground for five or six days and he then hears what he thinks is the rescue party. Jack dies and Stephen feels alone, but knocks against the wall with his knife to let them know he is there. After a further four hours' digging, it takes another five hours for the German soldiers to lay a charge to blast through the wall of chalk. Lamm detonates the charge to find the source of the tapping and they continue hacking at the walls. Stephen crawls out and he and Levi embrace. The German soldiers take Stephen to their trench, which is empty; they hear the sound of birds. They realise the war is over and Stephen lays his head on Levi's chest and sobs.

The German soldiers bury Jack with Joseph. Levi gives Stephen his belt buckle, and Stephen gives him his knife. Levi makes him promise he will write to him and they embrace. Part Six finishes with Stephen walking back across no-man's-land to the sound of a lark singing.

COMMENTARY

Because Stephen is rescued by enemy soldiers, the idea of war and enemies is questioned once again. This is emphasised further with the narrative focus on Levi and the death of his brother. The portrayal of these men means that the constructed enemy are given the human characteristics that were denied them in the propaganda that Stephen and the other soldiers would have been exposed to. There is a constant switch in the narrative between the British and German soldiers once the Germans hear Stephen's explosion. These shifts prolong the tension of Stephen's discovery as well as revealing how this faceless enemy that he has hated for so long has many narratives too.

When Stephen and Levi embrace, a form of closure is achieved. This tallies with the end of the war, described as: 'The dam had broken, the German army had been swept away' (p. 484). The burial of Joseph and Jack in a joint grave **symbolises** a new beginning where peace reigns, and the exchange of personal belongings by Stephen and Levi is a **metaphorical** mark of the end of four years of

 CHECK THE BOOK
Storm of Steel (1920) by Ernst Jünger is an early memoir about the First World War, written from the perspective of a German soldier.

hostilities. Although Levi knows that Stephen's blast killed Joseph, he still embraces him and later makes him promise to write. Both men demonstrate the possibility of peace and forgiveness, reiterating the concept that nothing is beyond redemption.

The peace is also signalled with Stephen's walk back across no-man's-land to the sound of a lark singing. The scene refers us back to the novel's title and implies the possibility that the metaphor for fear, which is the bird, has become a figurative reference for Stephen's love of nature and the idea of redemption. At this point, then, it is suggested but not stated directly that Stephen is able to look forward to the future rather than being trapped in a past from where his fear of birds originates.

> **GLOSSARY**
> 455 **sangfroid** literally 'cold blood'; coolness, especially under pressure
> 461 **guncotton** also known as nitrocellulose a form of explosive
> 482 *feldgrau* literally, 'field grey', the colour of the German uniforms

PART SEVEN: ENGLAND 1979

PAGES 487–503

- Elizabeth tells her mother that she is pregnant.
- Françoise tells Elizabeth that Isabelle was her real mother; not Jeanne.
- Françoise relates the stories of Isabelle and Stephen.
- Elizabeth gives birth with Robert present and she names the baby John.
- The novel ends with a reference to the sound of a crow.

CHECK THE POEM
Thomas Hardy's 'The Darkling Thrush' (1900) is a transitional poem that marks the turn of the century. Compare the use of birdsong in this poem with the end of Faulks's novel.

Part Seven is set in England, 1979. Elizabeth finishes reading the translations of Stephen's notebooks and takes particular notice of Stephen saying that he will have children for Jack. She has arranged to meet her mother to let her know about her pregnancy and is dubious about how Françoise will take the news because it means she will be an unmarried mother.

Elizabeth is surprised at how calm her mother is and Françoise explains how her parents were not married when she was born either. She then tells Elizabeth that Isabelle, and not Jeanne, was her biological mother and Elizabeth's grandmother. Isabelle died in the flu epidemic in 1919. She had decided that if anything should happen to her, she would like Jeanne to raise her daughter. This had been agreed between the two women when Isabelle first went to Germany. Max also agreed to this arrangement and died not long after from the injuries received in the war.

> **CONTEXT**
>
> The flu pandemic of 1918–19 is thought to have killed between 25 million and 50 million people around the world.

Françoise also tells Elizabeth how Stephen barely spoke for two years after the war and when he did he never mentioned it. He died at the age of 48, just before Françoise got married.

Elizabeth's contractions begin when she is in Dorset with Robert and she gives birth in the cottage with him present. She has a son and names him John in order to keep the promise Stephen made to Jack about having children for him. The novel ends with Robert, overjoyed at the birth, disturbing a crow roosting in a horse chestnut tree.

COMMENTARY

This final section marks a further tying up of ends as Françoise explains to Elizabeth about her grandparents and how Isabelle died in 1919. Added poignancy is given when Françoise tells Elizabeth that Stephen died at only 48 and she does not remember him ever discussing the war.

As this is a novel that is concerned with the connections between the past and present, it is worth noting that this theme is returned to finally when Elizabeth gives birth. By naming the baby John, Elizabeth keeps the promise that her grandfather made to Jack: because of this their memories are kept alive by the next generation.

The final 'harsh, ambiguous call' of the crow that Robert disturbs in the tree upholds the ambiguity of the title in relation to Stephen's

 QUESTION When Elizabeth names her son John, an attempt is made to unite the past with the present. How effective is this device?

fear of birds (p. 503). Whereas at the end of Part Six the sound of a bird was used to denote the possibility of peace, and of hope, the description of the sound of the crow is a shift back to a less optimistic view of nature and humanity's relationship with it. This ambiguity fits with the news that Stephen barely spoke for two years after the war. His silence demonstrates that although the hope of being able to move away from the past is necessary, it is not necessarily possible.

Through the adjective 'ambiguous', the ending reminds us of the continued relevance of the subject matter of war. The First World War was not the 'war to end all wars' as was hoped. With the continued disruptions to peace around the world, the sound of the crow acts as a **metaphor** for the ambivalent attitude of humanity towards war and conflict.

> **GLOSSARY**
>
> 497 **Braxton Something** Braxton Hicks contractions; false labour contractions

? QUESTION
In this extract, Stephen is **characterised** as being more instinctive than Isabelle. To what extent do you think this difference in temperament is based on their respective class positions and gender?

EXTENDED COMMENTARIES

TEXT 1 – PART ONE, PAGES 29–30

From 'He snipped at a few dead flowers ...' to ' ... some unwanted feeling.'

In this extract, Stephen approaches Isabelle in the garden at Amiens and the tension between them is described. At this point, they are still relatively formal with each other and Stephen tries to overcome this barrier between them with his physical proximity and dialogue.

Stephen has already taken the pruning shears from Isabelle. Faulks's description of Stephen snipping at the dead flowers without knowing what he is doing stands as an **allegory** for what happens later when they begin a sexual relationship. Stephen acts on instinct rather than forward planning while Isabelle is seen to be the one who takes the greater care about detail. This is demonstrated when she takes the shears from Stephen and shows him what to do.

Isabelle's awareness of propriety is prominent here because she appears to be determined to maintain her social standing. She colours when Stephen grabs her hand, and then asks him to let go of it and respect her position. It could be argued that when they make love this sense of propriety is abandoned: Stephen's instinctive awareness of her body gives Isabelle the chance to explore her sexuality with more freedom.

The language used in this passage is detailed in its descriptions and allows for a slow pace as Stephen makes an 'advance' on Isabelle. This heightens the tension between them and creates a closed atmosphere that echoes Stephen's feelings for her. Isabelle's clothing, for example, is dwelt upon as the third-person **narrator** examines her through Stephen's perspective and we are told that he moves closer to her in order to smell her: 'The little waistcoat she wore above it was open to reveal a rosy flush at the bottom of her throat, brought on by the small exertion of her gardening' (p. 29).

Adjectives are used more liberally here when compared to the sections set in the war (as Faulks explains in the Introduction), highlighting both the relatively sumptuous times of indolent peace before the fighting began as well as the difference in Stephen's outlook when compared to what it becomes in the trenches. His awareness of Isabelle demonstrates he has the leisure and wherewithal to look at her with such scrutiny.

There is, however, an undercurrent of violence in the Azaire household and Stephen's knowledge of this leads him to want to touch Isabelle in a protective way, and so treat her differently from the way Azaire does. The brutality Azaire inflicts on Isabelle is imagined by Stephen as 'her flesh beaten by her withered, corrupt husband' (p. 29). This exemplifies the impossible position she is in, as she is expected to endure such treatment as Azaire's wife, and is also a pre-cursor to the bodily violence that comes in the war scenes.

 QUESTION
How does Stephen's desire to protect Isabelle compare with Azaire's treatment of her? Does either man ever fully understand her?

TEXT 2 – PART TWO, PAGES 225–6

From 'The noise overhead ...' to 'Ten yards ahead and to the right was Colonel Barclay. He was carrying a sword.'

CHECK THE FILM

The final minutes of the television series *Blackadder Goes Forth* (1989), written by Richard Curtis and Ben Elton, encapsulate the moment when the men are ordered to go over the top. They are filmed in slow motion for a poignant effect.

This passage begins at 7.15 am on the first day of the Battle of the Somme, on 1 July 1916. It describes some of the tension before the men go over the top at 7.30 am and captures the early stages of the attack. It also depicts the ferocity and senselessness of that day.

Faulks describes the atmosphere prior to the attack as unbearably tense as the men wait for the signal to advance and make their various preparations for what is to come: 'The noise overhead began to intensify. Seven-fifteen. They were almost there. Stephen on his knees, some men taking photographs from their pockets, kissing the faces of their wives and children. Hunt telling foul jokes. Petrossian clasping a silver cross' (p. 225). The content of this quotation relates the dreadful anticipation that the men feel. The use of phrases and short sentences has the effect of enhancing the immediacy of the situation and contrasts with their ordinary lives. The references to the sounds of shells overhead emphasise their plight: 'The air overhead was packed solid with noise that did not move. It was as though waves were piling up in the air but would not break' (p. 225). The terror experienced is captured in Stephen's reaction ('It was like no sound on earth') and in his desperate appeals to a higher power (p. 225).

The length of sentences is also of note in the description of the scene moments before the attack starts. Here they are short. When Stephen finally blows the whistle and climbs up out of the trenches into no-man's-land, the sentences are comparatively long, emphasising the change in content, as the attack has begun. This may be interpreted as reflecting the surreal aspect of the situation: 'He clambered out and looked around him. It was for a moment completely quiet as the bombardment ended and the German guns also stopped. Skylarks wheeled and sang high in the cloudless sky. He felt alone, as though he had stumbled on this fresh world at the instant of its creation' (p. 225). This may also be interpreted as the calm before the man-made storm and the brutality of the violence to come.

The reference to a 'fresh world' is, like the title of the novel, used ironically. Both 'birdsong' and 'fresh world' might ordinarily be expected to denote optimism, hope and even innocence. In the context of this first day of the Battle of the Somme, however, some meanings are seen to change forever as the carnage that ensues has the effect of bringing in a new world of mass murder in a single day.

This passage makes several references to the tactical errors and outmoded orders that contributed to the extent of the number of men killed. It has been argued that the blowing-up of Hawthorn Ridge at 7.15 gave the Germans the signal to prepare for the forthcoming attack. Faulks tells of the order for the men to walk slowly, despite the machine-gun fire aimed at them, and describes Colonel Barclay walking ahead carrying a sword, illustrating the arrogant perspective of the commanding officers and strategists who failed to understand the mechanised nature of this war.

The lack of ownership that these soldiers had over their own lives, and the abuse of power that made them walking sacrifices, is described with the metaphor that refers to them as 'primitive dolls' with arms that flap as they go down after being shot (p. 226). Just like dolls, they have no autonomy over their actions – failing to follow orders is punishable by death. The word 'primitive' describes the senseless barbarity of the actions they are expected to undertake.

CHECK THE BOOK
R. C. Sherriff's *Journey's End* (1928) is a drama set in an officers' dugout in the British trenches of the First World War. It explores the physical and psychological impact of the war on the serving men over a few days in March 1918.

TEXT 3 – PART SIX, PAGES 470–3

From 'He flicked the blade open ...' to ' ... to give the rescue party guidance.'

This passage is set underground when Stephen and Jack are trapped after an explosion. It begins when Stephen contemplates cutting his own throat rather than die slowly and ends with Jack's death.

The use of direct speech gives us an insight into the perspectives of the characters away from the third-person narrator. In this case, Stephen's belief that he has never been loved and his explanation that this is why he is determined to survive are revealed and Jack's

hallucinatory state is made clear. Furthermore, Stephen's faith in
something other than the here and now is expanded upon: 'It was
as though I went through a door and beyond it there were sounds
and signals from some further existence' (p. 472). He explains that
this occurred as a result of his relationship with Isabelle, which in
turn articulates the strength of their bond.

Stephen's speech links us back to Part One of the novel, when he
went to stay with the Azaires. This has the effect of adding
poignancy to his predicament because we are reminded of his life
before the war. He describes himself as then being 'alive to
dangerous currents' and how at that age he had no fear. This may
also be seen as a generalised description of the millions of other
men who joined up to fight without knowing the consequences
(p. 472). The connection between the past and present **narratives**
demonstrates the changes Stephen has undergone as he has
matured, and shows how close he now is to death, trapped in this
claustrophobic tunnel.

A further connection to the past is made when Stephen holds the
knife to his throat. He begins to think of suicide as the only tenable
option, but reconsiders when he feels his pulse beating: 'He was
struck by its faithful indifference to everything but its own rhythm'
(p. 471). As well as making him think of his own past as a child in
Lincolnshire, we are alerted to an association with Isabelle in that
he referred to her as 'pulse' in Part One (p. 22). This pulse is a
motif for life: it is allotted to Stephen because although buried, as
Isabelle was **figuratively** in her marriage to Azaire, the pulse means
the possibility of escape.

QUESTION
How is the
tense atmosphere
in this extract
created? Take
account of the
language used,
the tone and
characterisation.

The passage ends with Jack coming closer to dying and with
Stephen continuing to try to alert the rescue party that he is still
there. Faulks describes the continuance of life in the midst of death
and **characterises** Stephen as heroic while he refuses to submit to
his circumstances: 'Stephen began to knock rhythmically with the
end of his knife against the wall of chalk by his head to give the
rescue party guidance' (p. 473). As is in keeping with a work
concerned with war and survival, the main **protagonist** perseveres
as he attempts to make contact with others.

TEXT 4 – PART SEVEN, PAGES 501–3

From 'Robert stood up and went through into the kitchen ... ' to 'Now here was John, his boy, another chance.'

In this passage, Elizabeth gives birth to her son John (in 1979) with the help of her lover, Robert. The birth scene brings the novel to a close and the continuation of the bloodline of Stephen's family **symbolises** a faith in renewal. Faulks's description of the birth is a further example of the 'flesh and blood' that has dominated the novel.

The **imagery** used to depict the birth is graphic and as with the portrayal of sex (in Part One) and of the carnage in the war scenes, Faulks is unflinching in his descriptions of the body and its functions. The new-born baby is described: 'Its skin was grey and covered with a whiteish substance, thick and greasy about the chest and back'; the umbilical cord is referred to as 'angry purple'; and we are told the baby 'slithered' into Robert's hands in 'a rush of blood' (p. 502).

> **QUESTION**
> What is the effect of using such vivid imagery in the descriptions of death and birth in this instance?

Once more, Faulks avoids a sentimental tone in order to portray the action (of the birth) with **realism**. While giving birth, Elizabeth becomes a force of nature, 'of muscle, instinct and willpower', and through this description her strength is recognised (p. 502). The reference to instinct is also an indirect **allusion** to Stephen as a young man in Part One when he preferred to be instinctive rather than plan ahead.

This passage also contains the moment when Elizabeth names her son John in order to keep Stephen's promise to Jack. By keeping this promise, which she learned of through reading Stephen's notebooks, she maintains the bond between the two men as well the connection she desires with her own past (to Stephen that is). It is also telling that Robert feels as though he is living 'on the edge of death and drama' compared to their neighbours, who are 'calmly asleep' in the nearby village (p. 501). This may be linked in part to Stephen's experiences in the war and the oblivion of those at home.

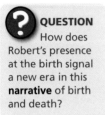

QUESTION
How does Robert's presence at the birth signal a new era in this **narrative** of birth and death?

A link between Robert and Stephen is evident in the epiphany Robert experiences at the birth of his son: 'The feeling that rose up inside him was like taking flight; his spirit ... seemed to soar into the air' (p. 503). This sensation is comparable with Stephen's experience of 'binding love' on his home leave to Norfolk during the war (p. 363). In both instances, these men are sited in the natural environment. Their love for the world around them lends the novel a sign of the possibility, at least, of the redemption of humanity.

PART THREE

CRITICAL APPROACHES

CHARACTERISATION

When studying the development of characters and analysing their characterisation we must remember that they have been constructed by the author of the work. We must avoid falling into the trap of thinking of these characters as real people and we must always consider how the author causes them to interact with each other and determines the roles each of the characters plays.

The characters of a novel are developed through a number of means, including physical descriptions and background information. In *Birdsong*, the majority of the details about the characters are revealed in the third person, as in the commentary about Isabelle's formative years in Part One (pp. 34–8). The thoughts and memories of characters also help to develop their identities, as when Stephen thinks about his childhood home (pp. 115–16) and when Jack cannot recall the face of his son to draw it (p. 372). The latter example demonstrates Jack's grief as well as the damage inflicted by the war. Dialogue is relevant for examining characterisation because this shows us how characters respond to each other, and may reveal gaps between what they feel and what they say. Letters are also of interest because they are first-person accounts that may give details of a character's emotional state. In *Birdsong*, however, it is more likely that they show characters hiding the truth, for example when Jack and Jeanne write to their loved ones telling them not to worry.

STEPHEN

Stephen is the central protagonist. His stay with the Azaires in 1910 and his subsequent affair with Isabelle, as well as his numerous experiences in the war, are paramount concerns in the novel. He is depicted as diffident and peculiar in his behaviour towards others when he is first shown at war in 1916: 'He was not a popular officer. He found it difficult to think of words of encouragement or inspiration when he himself did not believe there was a purpose to

QUESTION
What changes does Stephen undergo during the war? Analyse how he develops from 1910 until the end of the war.

the war or an end to it in sight' (p. 145). Because we are gradually given an insight into his background and emotions in Part One of the novel it is evident that the formation of his character is dependant on his sense of abandonment by both his mother and then Isabelle. While the futility of the war colours his personality, it is telling that his two lovers, Isabelle and Jeanne, are both older than him. These relationships suggest that as an adult he continues to search for the love he failed to receive from his mother.

Stephen is also consistently drawn as passionate; he prefers to act instinctively rather than think through the consequences of his actions. This is evident in his relationship with Isabelle and when he takes Weir to visit prostitutes. We first see Stephen as a young, single man with few worries. As he experiences the loss of Isabelle when she leaves him, and witnesses the carnage of war, however, it is possible to see him pass through stages of diffidence, fear and finally a subdued optimism at the end of the war. He also has an almost mystical experience on his home leave in Norfolk, when he feels a sense of 'binding love', and it is telling that he returns to this county when the war is over (p. 363).

As a sign of Stephen's importance to *Birdsong*, his background is the most developed of the characters. His fear of birds is a constant reminder of the title because it undermines the supposed innocence that is usually evoked by the word. For him, birdsong is a mark of his long-held phobia rather than an unambiguous reference to the beauty of nature. The phobia distinguishes him as once more not belonging to the rest of society, as he is frightened by what others take pleasure in. This is also an indicator of how much his childhood still influences his behaviour as an adult.

CHECK THE BOOK

In Charles Dickens's *Great Expectations* (1861), the life of orphan Pip is altered after the intervention of a benefactor.

Stephen's lonely childhood is revealed gradually and this is in keeping with his characteristic sense of independence and dislike of explaining himself to others. We are told that his mother and father were not married and when she fell pregnant 'he disappeared' (p. 103). She went on to abandon him too after meeting another man and Stephen was brought up by his grandparents and then sent to an institution. Vaughan stepped in as a benefactor and ensured that Stephen had a good education, but according to Stephen he showed him no love.

With this background, Stephen is made into an archetype of the orphan who has no ties and is open to adventures (see **Background: Literary background**). Faulks's depiction of Stephen as an adult explores what might happen to such a child hero of literature as he grows up. When in the tunnel with Jack in Part Six, for instance, Stephen explains how he has always felt unloved: 'No one had ever loved me. That's the truth of it, though I wasn't aware of it then. I wasn't like you with your mother. No one cared where I was or whether I should live or die' (p. 472). Despite or because of this, Stephen goes on to tell Jack that he has had to come up with his 'own reasons for living' and will 'chew [his] way out like a rat' if he has to (p. 472).

Stephen's origins are working-class: he is described as a Lincolnshire farm boy several times as though this overrides the education he received courtesy of Vaughan. However, this education has had the effect of giving him an insight into, if not a place in, middle-class society and plays a part in his promotion from the ranks. Faulks describes Stephen as not belonging fully to any of the roles he plays, making him an isolated central figure.

In terms of the plot, Stephen's knowledge of Greek and Latin adds an element of mystery because he is able to use it to write in code in his secret notebooks. As it takes Bob months to decode them, it is apparent that Stephen has successfully manipulated his education for his own purpose. The references to Greek and Latin conjure up a connection between him and the distant past, and remind us once more of how strong the influence of history is on the present in this novel. This education also gave him the means to control his openness as he was growing up: 'This sense of secrecy was something he had had to cultivate in order to overcome a natural openness and a quick temper' (p. 15). As a child he went on to learn 'to wait and be watchful' and he sees this as being a result of the education he received under Vaughan's direction (p. 15).

Stephen is alone again after Isabelle leaves him and this is the reason Faulks gives for him joining up to fight in the war. He is 'relieved' when it starts and it is suggested that this is because of 'the sudden chill loss of her' (p. 161). It is explicitly stated that the new enemy became the focus of his emotions: 'The suppressed frustrations and unexpressed violence of his life were turned into hatred of the Germans' (p. 161).

 CHECK THE BOOK

The Great Gatsby (1925) by F. Scott Fitzgerald is a novel set in the aftermath of the First World War and portrays the effects of the war on American society, as well as being a story of doomed love.

STEPHEN continued

Because of Stephen's centrality to the novel, his experience of the war dominates the war scenes. The focus shifts temporarily to others such as Jack and Weir in particular, but Stephen attracts the greatest attention. His injuries are detailed, as is the part he plays in the attacks on the enemy. He is the only one rescued from the tunnel in the penultimate section and because he has been followed throughout, we are given some satisfaction in the midst of the carnage because he at least survives. The pleasure is tempered with the news that he hardly speaks for two years after the war and dies at the relatively young age of 48. His daughter, Françoise, explains that the war had a lasting impact: 'Like a lot of men of that generation, he never really recovered' (p. 494).

Despite his main role, little else is revealed about what happened to Stephen after his rescue. This may be interpreted as a means of keeping the focus on the war rather than his reactions to it. Françoise recalls her father with love; she explains how they lived in Norfolk when she was a child, at the time when he was slowly recovering his speech. This means he returned to the county where he first felt an affinity with nature and gained the knowledge that redemption is possible. It is fitting that this place became his home because this is where he first experiences what it is to belong.

CHECK THE BOOK

Gustave Flaubert's famous novel, *Madame Bovary* (1857), tells the story of a young middle-class wife in a loveless marriage, who finds solace in an affair with a young student. Like Isabelle, Emma Bovary rebels against a social role that gives her very little freedom: it was not until 1944 that women in France were granted the vote.

ISABELLE

Isabelle is characterised by her repressed passion, and in Part One we learn that she has remained in a loveless marriage largely because of convention and duty. She is described as being dressed well, in accordance with her position in society, and precise in her movements. Stephen considers her to be 'more fashionable' than other women in the town, but her clothes 'revealed less' (p. 22). Links may be made between her and the eponymous heroine Madame Bovary in that she is a provincial French wife who seeks more than she has been allotted.

This work is primarily concerned with the First World War and the impact this had on the men involved and so it is perhaps not surprising that female characters appear less frequently than their male counterparts. Isabelle, Elizabeth and Jeanne are the most prominent female characters, but even then they take minor roles in comparison to Stephen and, it could be argued, are used mainly to explain his experiences.

Faulks supplies insights into Isabelle's childhood and adolescence on pages 34–8. Her early years are described as oppressive because of her father's disappointment that he did not have a son. Her parents showed a general indifference to their children: 'He would rebuke the girls for bad behaviour and occasionally punish them severely, but he had no other interest in their development. Madame Fourmentier was driven by his indifference into an excessive concern with fashion and appearance' (p. 35). Despite this lack of love, Isabelle is described as being good-natured and at 18 as 'a self-reliant but gentle girl who had no proper outlet either for her natural instincts or for the exuberant energy that was frustrated by the routine and torpor of her parents' house' (p. 36).

When Stephen meets Isabelle as a lodger in her home, she is married to Azaire and is clearly unhappy. Through his close observations and Isabelle's confidences, Azaire's violence towards her is explained as is her tolerance of it. She is a provincial middle-class woman of the period and because of this status, her religion (Catholicism) and the social mores of the time she is seemingly trapped forever in this relationship.

As Stephen watches her, we are given a perspective of Isabelle that is coloured by his desire for her, including the minutiae of her movements and clothing. He notices the flush on her cheek when she sees him look at her; when he comes to her in the garden as she prunes the roses he observes her character by the clothes she wears. Her skirt is described as being the colour of 'parched earth' and her blouse has 'dog-toothed edging'. Her attire reminds him of 'victory balls', highlighting her wealth and position in relation to him as well as his high opinion of her (p. 29). At this point, she is aloof in her role as a married woman with two step-children and is always of a different class to Stephen. With him, though, she is able to experience the sense of freedom that Jeanne first inspired in her as a young woman. Jeanne taught her to believe there should be no restrictions in the way she acts, and it is in Isabelle's affair with Stephen that she has the opportunity to follow this advice.

CHECK THE BOOK

For further insights into the role women played in the First World War, see the anthology, *The Virago Book of Women and the Great War* (1999), edited by Joyce Marlow. It includes recorded memories of women in Britain, the USA, Russia and mainland Europe.

When Isabelle finally tells Azaire of her affair with Stephen, she voices her feelings with regard to both men and explains that in truth she does not know how either feels about her. She follows this with an impassioned speech where she demands that Azaire appreciate her as an individual: 'I'm a frightened woman, no more than that – not an adulterer, or a harlot or anything else. I'm just the same person I ever was, but you never took the trouble to find out what that was' (p. 97).

Isabelle leaves Stephen after she discovers she is pregnant because she begins to believe their relationship is a sin and is afraid of the possibility of a miscarriage. Religion is tied to despair as she leaves him in the hope that this will save her baby. Furthermore, she is aware of Stephen's distance from his own life, and his independence, and wonders if this will affect her baby's future.

Isabelle's last appearance in the novel comes when Stephen meets her at her home and he notices how she has been permanently scarred by her injury from a shell. Their relationship is severed forever as she decides not to tell him about their daughter, but does let him know about her new lover, Max. Her reasoning is that if he knows about their child, 'it would make matters more painful and complicated between them' (p. 332), and telling him about Max 'would make things simpler and more final' (p. 333).

AZAIRE

In 1910, Azaire is described as a wealthy owner of factories and his home is an impressive display of wealth. Faulks describes him as possibly being 40, 'but could have been ten years more' and his eyes are described as having 'an alert, humourless glare' (p. 6).

QUESTION
What is the effect of Azaire's absence after Part One? Does this mimic his loss of power?

Azaire is the patriarch of his businesses and household; he is given no endearing qualities at this point. His violent treatment of his wife typifies his general brutality as well as his characteristic insecurity. Isabelle's description of him shows her ability to empathise while also demonstrating his disregard for her feelings: 'He seemed to build up this disgust with himself. It made him talk to me sarcastically. Perhaps you've noticed. He began to criticize me all the time when other people were here. I think that for some reason he felt guilty about marrying me' (p. 76). The guilt she perceives is linked to his marriage to her after the death of his first wife. Azaire's friendship with Bérard confirms his unpleasant character, however, because he belittles Isabelle in front of this least sympathetic character in the novel. The secret looks the two men share are further evidence of this, suggesting that Azaire has told Bérard about his troubled relationship with Isabelle.

Azaire does not appear after Part One, but because of the later explanation about what happens to him during the German occupation, which is given by Isabelle, Faulks allows him some redeeming qualities. He is now drawn as courageous, unselfish and even brave. This is because, as Isabelle tells Stephen, he sacrificed himself first as a hostage and then by volunteering for deportation to Germany: 'Although his age made him the object of several offers of release, he was steadfast in his determination to be with the wronged people of his town' (p. 332). This change in character is also signalled in the 'quite meek' manner with which he accepted Isabelle back, suggesting a desire to atone for his earlier sins (p. 330).

Such an alteration in Azaire's attitude towards Isabelle specifically and the people of the town more generally could be seen as too abrupt to be realistic. However, if we consider the desire for redemption that empowers Stephen to survive the last stages of the war, this change for the better in Azaire may be construed as an example of the possibility of finding virtue, as well as evidence of the life-changing effects of war.

LISETTE AND GRÉGOIRE AZAIRE

As with their father and Bérard, Lisette and Grégoire appear only in Part One; they are merely referred to in passing in later sections. Lisette is the older of the two and has her dark hair in ribbons when Stephen first meets her. Stephen presumes she is aged about 16, Grégoire around 10 (p. 5). At the family's first meal with Stephen, Lisette tells a story to show that she is beyond childish concerns, but seems 'unsure' where her own interests lie (p. 6). Both children are minor characters, but Lisette's flirtation with Stephen gives her slightly greater input and more depth. She threatens to blackmail him when he rejects her on the fishing trip,

QUESTION
How does Lisette's flirtation with Stephen serve to highlight his passion for Isabelle?

adding some tension to the relationship between Stephen and Isabelle. This situation also demonstrates her desire to be seen as an adult although she is not quite fully mature.

As Lisette and Grégoire grow older, details of their lives are filtered through to Stephen. He is informed that Lisette married Lucien Lebrun, who, ironically, Stephen had been jealous of. In 1917, Grégoire is preparing to join up the following year if the war is still on (p. 335). It is also partly because of their pleading that Isabelle returns to Azaire. Without their intervention, Isabelle's return may not have taken place, given the reasons she left and the freedom she found.

BÉRARD

Bérard is described as 'a heavily set grey-haired man in his fifties' (p. 7). He is significant because of his friendship with Azaire. He has no redeeming traits and, on his visits to the Azaire home, he is seen to be domineering when he takes over the conversation and attempts to belittle Isabelle. It transpires that he knows of Azaire's violent treatment of her, and this is illustrated in the looks of complicity that pass between the two friends, and in Isabelle's view that her husband discusses his humiliation of her. Stephen regards Bérard with disdain, but also recognises the power he likes to exert over others: 'He was only a small-town bully, it was true, but he was clearly used to having his own way' (p. 10).

QUESTION
Bérard is a reminder that not everybody performs heroically in war situations. Is he the only exception?

Unlike Azaire, who goes on to perform heroically during the German occupation of Amiens, Bérard becomes a collaborator when he offers his home up to the German commandant. His malevolence is seen to be unchanging because he also informs Isabelle's parents of her relationship with Max.

JACK FIREBRACE

Jack is introduced abruptly in the novel at the beginning of Part Two where he is working underground as a tunneller. He used to work in the construction of the London underground and his previous skills are brought to bear on this job. Jack is characterised as being an artist and the joker among the men he works with, making him one of the more developed characters. He is also one of the few fathers in the novel who demonstrates love for his son:

he has been given the role of the family man in the narrative. Jack's care for his child may be seen as a counterpoint to Azaire's role as a father when Stephen first encounters him in Part One. As with many of the men, Jack's letters home (to his wife) exhibit a protective love to her as he refuses to tell her the worst of his experiences. Through Jack, one of the older men among the tunnellers and infantry, Faulks is able to give an insight into the experience of the father and husband serving in the war. He is also the vehicle for Faulks's descriptions of the impact of the war on ordinary men. As a manual worker earning little money before the war, he is embarrassed that the food is better in the trenches than it often was at home (p. 142).

Jack and Weir are described by Faulks as being used as a counterpoint to Stephen: 'Michael Weir and Jack Firebrace provided harmonic lines in counterpoint to Stephen's: innocent when he is worldly, scared where he is cold, despondent while he remains questing' (Introduction, p. xiv). In other words, Faulks has used them to distinguish the characterisation of Stephen: the counterpoint becomes more apparent when these men share the same scenes. Jack's contact with Stephen begins when Stephen threatens to put him on a charge for sleeping on duty. He goes on to save Stephen when he is presumed dead. Stephen, in turn, tries to save Jack when they are trapped in the tunnel in Part Six.

Jack's spirituality is also a part of his make-up: it is his decision to say a prayer for Stephen that leads him to find Stephen among the dead. Due to his faith Jack suffers hurt when he questions it. This occurs on the day Jack sees the padre throw down his cross in disgust at the carnage they witness, and he explains this shortly before he dies: 'What I've seen ... I don't want to live any more. That day you attacked. We watched you. Me and Shaw. The padre, that man, can't remember his name. If you'd seen, you'd understand. Tore his cross off' (p. 471). The speech is broken to reflect how close to death he is, but it also heightens the effect the events have had on him. The use of phrases rather than sentences makes his point direct and urgent. He continues to tell Stephen how the horrors he has witnessed mean he knows the world is no place for his son to live in: 'My boy, gone. What a world we made for him. I'm glad he's dead. I'm *glad*' (p. 471).

QUESTION
How effective is the use of 'counterpoint' with regard to Jack and Stephen in the novel?

Earlier in the novel, when Jack thinks he is going to be court-martialled for sleeping on duty, his thoughts of impending death are described. Because of the development given to his character at this early stage – we know some details of his home life for example – we are driven to feel empathy for him. He has learned to be pragmatic about the death of the enemy and even friends at this point, but he recognises he is not 'indifferent to the prospect of his own death' (p. 131). He is also ashamed to admit to himself that he would rather others die instead of him. By the time he is trapped in the tunnel in Part Six, he has come to regard his death as more welcome than being alive to suffer the pity of others.

MICHAEL WEIR

Weir is one of Stephen's few friends. This friendship is strengthened because he is also one of the few to have gone through so many stages of the war. Weir and Stephen make their war experiences bearable for each other. Weir joined the Royal Engineers in 1912 and this meant his loneliness while growing up was somehow alleviated: 'I liked having a role. And I liked the comradeship. It was as simple as that. I had no friends before, and suddenly I found that I had, if not the friendship then at least the company of hundreds of men my age' (pp. 153–4).

CHECK THE BOOK
Heartbreak House (1919) by George Bernard Shaw **satirises** the middle classes and the part they played in the build-up to war.

Weir is also depicted as an innocent despite the length of his service and the horrors he has seen. This innocence is emphasised by the information that he is virgin and the thought of having sex with a woman has become more complicated as the years go on. Stephen attempts to free him from this anxiety by taking him to a brothel, but this only underlines Weir's worries as the prostitute reveals that he cried while he was with her.

The description of Weir's return home to his parents demonstrates the alienation that he and others like him now feel as their outlook is disfigured by the experience of war. The barrier between him and his parents, who are also a **metaphor** for the general public away from the front line, appears to be insurmountable. Weir is unable to find the words to explain, and his parents are unwilling to ask. This is captured in the conversation he has with his father: 'Weir wondered if he was going to say any word of greeting. By the time they reached the French windows to the sitting room it was clear that the moment had passed' (p. 287).

Weir's isolation is signified further by his appearance and behaviour. Our first glimpse of Captain Weir shows his appearance to be unconventional: Faulks describes him as 'a startling figure with disarrayed hair, in plimsolls and civilian sweater' (p. 122). As the war progresses he drinks alcohol copiously and his hands shake. It is never fully explained if the shaking is due solely to the shock of war, as in the effects of shell-shock, or if *delirium tremens* (where the 'tremens' is associated with alcoholism) also plays a part. Either way, while alive he becomes a walking casualty as fear overtakes him. Stephen explains to Ellis that this is not the fear one might expect: 'He's not afraid of gas or shells or being buried. He's frightened that it doesn't make sense, that there is no purpose. He's afraid that he has somehow strayed into the wrong life' (p. 309). The sensitivity that has made him a lonely figure prior to the war threatens his sanity while on the front line, and yet he is still seen to persevere with the expectations placed on him. This includes his willingness to continue going down into the tunnels despite his anxieties.

CHECK THE BOOK

The influence of the First World War on Freud may be seen in *Civilization and Its Discontents* (1930). In this work, he looks at the individual and society from a pessimistic perspective.

GRAY

When Elizabeth makes a telephone call to Gray, a voice is given to the past. As with Brennan, he acts as a conduit for Elizabeth's research and, in terms of the novel, he is a present-day witness to Stephen's life in the war. He is also a link with *Charlotte Gray*, the third work in Faulks's trilogy, as he is the father of the eponymous heroine.

CHECK THE FILM

Charlotte Gray (2001) is an adaptation of Faulks's novel of the same title and is set during the Second World War. It is both a drama and romance and the heroine, who is played by Cate Blanchett, is the daughter of Captain Gray of *Birdsong*.

As Stephen's commanding officer, Gray wills him and others to continue fighting and advises Stephen to make his men love him: 'They'll fight better' (p. 162). He also urges Stephen to try to think past the events they have seen and remember the future. Stephen sees Gray on the first day of the Battle of the Somme as he orders the men to go over the top, and later recalls the look in his eyes as one of 'perfect blankness' (p. 341). Stephen understands this as representing the same void in his soul that he has.

Faulks describes Gray as 'unorthodox' in that although he is strict he is aware of the need to support the men under him. His interest in literature and psychology contributes to this understanding of him, as does the brief mention of his upbringing: 'A childhood in the Scottish Lowlands had given him a dry sense of mockery and tempered his more abstract military and psychological theories with practical caution' (p. 163). He is influenced by psychoanalysis in his interpretation of Stephen's interest in superstition, marking him as widely read as well as representing the growing interest in this field at the time.

BRENNAN

Brennan is a minor character in the war sections. He carries the dead body of his brother back from no-man's-land and tells Stephen how lucky he is to have missed the first day of the Battle of the Somme, having been blown off the fire-step before the attack. This scene between Brennan and Stephen is significant not only for its poignancy, but also because Brennan appears again in 1978 when Elizabeth visits him. The damage he has suffered is seen to have lasted a lifetime.

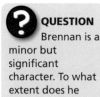

QUESTION
Brennan is a minor but significant character. To what extent does he connect the past with the present?

Faulks uses Brennan as a living enactment of the war: as with Gray, he is a witness to those times. He has been neglected as one of the forgotten casualties and this is made literal as we are told he has had no visitors for thirty years. By including him in these later sections, he and others like him are commemorated. Brennan's mind is confused and he is physically disabled because one of his legs has been amputated. He is a testament to the other forgotten young men injured during the war as well as the dead. In the tunnel before his death, Jack tells Stephen that he would rather die than end up this way: 'Not for me. In a home, with no legs. I don't want their pity' (p. 471).

ELLIS

Ellis is a young subaltern aged 19 or 20 in 1917. He acts as a comparison to explain how the war has ravaged its long-term participants, such as Weir, Jack and Stephen. In this light, he is an innocent because of his lack of experience as well as his age. The disbelief that Weir shows when Ellis says he is fighting to win the war for 'our country' allows us to compare the outlook of the one who is battle hardened and now unpatriotic with one who is relatively naive about the nature of this war (p. 293). He is also a means of introducing some energy to the narrative because he encourages Stephen to visit Amiens with him, leading smoothly to Stephen's encounter with Jeanne.

Ellis's death adds yet another layer of poignancy because Stephen knows that he must write to his mother to inform her of the news. At first, Stephen wants to write in a personal style, but opts for 'formal words of condolence' as he has for other relatives of dead soldiers in his platoon (p. 382). His death is one of many that Stephen has had to explain; he knows that with time his style has become 'dry and passionless' and he cannot bring himself to consider the effects such a letter will have on the recipient: 'Her only son gone … He did not wish to contemplate it' (p. 383).

ELIZABETH

Elizabeth is the central focus of the modern-day narrative much as her grandfather, Stephen, is at the heart of the war sections. At the beginning of her story, we learn that Elizabeth is having an affair with a married man (Robert). She is introduced to Stuart, by her friend Lindsay, so that she might become attached to somebody with whom she could settle down and have a family. Elizabeth is now 38 and has up to this point been concentrating on her career; as her story progresses, however, she becomes increasingly preoccupied with the idea of having children. Indeed, as with Isabelle, the desire to be a mother comes to dominate her characterisation.

Elizabeth is depicted initially as a blank slate with regard to the First World War. She is used to represent those who are entirely ignorant of the events of this era, and her search for what happened historically as well as to discover more about Stephen is crucial to her character and to the narrative. This storyline is made plausible as her lack of knowledge means that she must follow up the clues to Stephen's background and details of the First World War to understand him and herself more fully: 'Beginning with the contents of her mother's attic she would track this man down … It

QUESTION
How does Ellis's appearance highlight the disenchantment of Weir and Stephen?

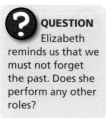

QUESTION
Elizabeth reminds us that we must not forget the past. Does she perform any other roles?

would be one way, at least, of understanding more about herself' (p. 250). Her interest is triggered by an article on the sixtieth anniversary of the Armistice; her lack of knowledge leads her colleague Erich to wonder about how good her schooling was. The shame she feels for not knowing more, and the shock she experiences at the Thiepval memorial, mean that she represents those who have not seen the relevance of history until this point. Through her, we are encouraged to see the past as belonging to the present and are reminded of the necessity of knowing what has gone before.

Elizabeth's pregnancy reiterates the **theme** of regeneration that has emerged intermittently in the war sections. The birth of her son signals the continuity with the past that she has searched for in the attic when looking for information concerning Stephen. By naming him John, the continuation is made concrete because she is keeping Stephen's promise to Jack. The birth also suggests the optimism that comes with the idea of rebirth and renewal and echoes the concept that nothing is beyond redemption. Life is seen to be a form of an antidote to the killings that are inherent to the war sections. In this case, blood and the anatomisation of the body are **symbols** for renewal rather than death.

JEANNE

Jeanne is one of Isabelle's older sisters; she is the one Isabelle loved most when growing up. When Jeanne first encounters Stephen she is wary of him, but she comes to trust and then love him. She has 'large, brown eyes', almost translucent skin and her voice is described as being 'low and soft' (p. 319). Compared to Isabelle, Jeanne's face is 'more strongly and simply constructed' (p. 319).

Although Jeanne goes on to be Stephen's lover, her influence is more subtle than active in that she acts as a support to others rather than having a decisive role to play. She is depicted as the stronger, more independent and older sister who encouraged Isabelle to challenge the oppression of their childhood home and wider society. Isabelle loved her for her 'humour and detachment' and because she 'gave Isabelle the feeling that the things she had read about in books and newspapers were not just the ingredients of other people's lives, as she had once believed, but were open to her to some extent too' (p. 36).

Jeanne also builds up Stephen's morale when she writes to him and when he visits her. She reminds him of the possibility of redemption and that the war is almost over. Her insights give Stephen some hope and prompt him to remember that there is a future. Like Isabelle, Jeanne is also older than Stephen and because of this, and because of the way she cares for him, she becomes a mother-figure too. Her love is nurturing and protective, an aspect of her character that is reiterated in her early relationship with Isabelle and later care for Françoise.

Jeanne's photograph is on display in the third story, set in the 1970s, and Elizabeth has always believed her to be her grandmother. Because of the photograph and the references to it, she is not entirely overlooked in the story about Stephen and Isabelle and is given a place in the family history.

CHECK THE BOOK
French Women and the First World War (2000) by Margaret Darrow gives an insight into how French women lived through the war.

LEVI

Levi is a lieutenant in the German army and a children's doctor in civilian life. He plays only a minimal role in the novel, when he leads Lamm and Kroger to find his brother Joseph and then Stephen, but he is particularly relevant for giving the enemy a human face. Until meeting Levi, Stephen has regarded the enemy with a hatred that has enabled him to continue fighting. His first sight of Levi reminds him of this: 'He looked up and saw the legs of his rescuer. They were clothed in the German *feldgrau*, the colour of his darkest dreams' (p. 482). The two men embrace and form a bond that **figuratively** represents the end of the war and signals a hope for future peace. Levi is a German Jewish man, however, and we as readers will understand the terrible **irony** of his hopes and his love for what he calls his fatherland. His re-appearance in *Charlotte Gray* highlights this.

FRANÇOISE

As with Jeanne, Françoise is a minor character – the daughter of Stephen and the mother of Elizabeth. Faulks uses her to explain the outcome of the lives of Stephen and Isabelle when Elizabeth reveals

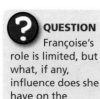

QUESTION
Françoise's role is limited, but what, if any, influence does she have on the narrative?

to her that she is pregnant in Part Seven. Although she barely features in the novel, Françoise is important as both the living connection between the two central characters and as a mother who has continued the bloodline, which is a significant aspect of Elizabeth's characterisation.

THEMES

WAR

The First World War is the dominant theme in the novel and, more specifically, the action on the Western Front is central to the plot. Even when scenes are not set in the 1914–18 time-frame, the narrative revolves around the war. For example, when Stephen and the Azaire family visit the Somme water-gardens in 1910 we recognise straightaway that a reference is being made to the tragic battleground of the years to come. In addition, his visit to Amiens cathedral and premonition of mass death is a reference to the forthcoming war. Similarly, the First World War is Elizabeth's focus in the 1970s as she searches the past to understand herself more.

Faulks's depiction of the tunnellers and underground tunnel system means that the First World War is explored from a new perspective. The battles in the tunnels and the conditions endured there give new insights and broaden our understanding of war and its effects. The relevance of the tunnelling work is also discussed, particularly when Gray questions the efficacy of it; for example, Faulks describes a rivalry between the infantry and the tunnellers, the 'sewer rats' (p. 128). However, the infantry and tunnellers are brought together as they are forced to defend one another.

In the sections set on the Western Front, the narrative immerses the readers in the atmosphere of fear and horror. This is at its most compelling when the unbearable tension before the first day of the Battle of the Somme is described (see **Extended commentaries: Text 2**). The graphic depictions of injuries and deaths ensure its realism.

Faulks captures the isolation that the men feel – both because of geography and because of the things they have seen and done.

When Weir and then Stephen go back to England on leave, they each notice how unwilling people are to understand what they have been through. This isolation is made literal in the scenes when Stephen and Jack are trapped in the tunnel with little hope of being rescued. It is also described when Jack considers how separated they are from the rest of society, even after Shaw has told him that on certain days the sound of the guns can be heard as far away as London: 'The place in which he often found himself, often underground, with no clear idea of where the nearest village was, seemed as distant from those streets and houses as if he now inhabited another world' (p. 128).

The war is understood as precipitating a break from the past and its certainties, demonstrated, for example, when Weir clings to Stephen at the end of the first day of the Battle of the Somme and asks 'What have we done? What have we done' (p. 239). The loss of life, made possible by improved technology, is graphically illustrated, as is the loss of hope for humanity. Stephen is constantly asked to keep a faith in the future, but his counterpoint, Jack, reflects the view of many that he does not want to live in the new world. The description of Brennan's 'existence' (rather than life) in the 1970s underlines the continuing devastating effects of war long after peace is declared.

LOVE

The novel presents us with a range of constructions of love and what it means to be loved (or not). The passionate love between Stephen and Isabelle is a central concern. There is also the love between men on the front line as well as the child's love for his or her mother. The first love for the mother is shown to be the last too for the soldiers when they are dying.

The lead-up to and outcome of the relationship between Stephen and Isabelle dominate Part One. This gives the narrative its central romantic storyline and highlights a connection between desire and death, which is continued into the war narrative. These twin drives are described as being bound up in each other and the theme of love introduces us to the carnage that comes in the war.

 CHECK THE POEM
In its form and content, the modernist poem 'The Waste Land' (1922) by T. S. Eliot captures the post-war fragmentation of certainties.

Stephen's relationship with Jeanne is less passionate and is one that is founded on the wreckage of destructive forces. This reflects an alteration of Stephen's outlook, as he matures, but perhaps also demonstrates a need for care and protection that Jeanne offers him (see **Characterisation: Jeanne** for more on her role in the novel).

CHECK THE BOOK

Eve Kosofsky Sedgwick's *Between Men: English Literature and Male Homosocial Desire* (1985) examines the bonds between men in literature. She points out how these bonds may come at the expense of the woman in a triangulated relationship.

The love between men is also drawn upon as a strong thematic concern. Homosexuality is not explicitly mentioned, but rather this love is depicted through scenes of camaraderie and the grief felt for those who have died. Jack's mourning for Shaw and Stephen's sense of loss when Weir dies are the two most detailed examples, but we should also remember the story of Brennan and how he picks up the corpse of his dead brother in no-man's-land to take him back behind the British lines to ensure he is buried. Love in war is described as dangerous because it means when one of the men dies the living will be weakened with grief again. Jack, for example, remembers this after the death of Shaw: 'I have made this mistake in my life, Jack thought: not once but twice I have loved someone more than my heart would bear' (p. 345)

The love for the mother is an undercurrent in the depiction of Stephen and his feelings of abandonment. This love is also referred to when men are seen to cry for their mothers when they are close to dying and is tied to a sense of endless loss. When Stephen is badly injured, he fears dying alone and his thoughts return to his mother. He also notices that Jack makes the same primitive sound he did when he called for his mother in his delirium: 'Jack began to moan softly. Stephen had heard the sound many times; it was a low, primitive cry he himself had made when he was carried in to the surgeon. Jack was calling to his mother' (pp. 455–6).

HISTORY AND ITS CONNECTION TO THE PRESENT

The significance of the past and the need to remember it is necessarily present in a work that has the First World War at its centre. By default, we as readers are forced to remember these men and cannot help but consider the lasting impression the war had on this generation of men and women.

This theme is further emphasised with the use of Elizabeth Benson in the 1978–79 sections and with the related theme of redemption. We and Elizabeth are asked not only to remember the past, but also to understand what happened. That is, the presence of history is used as a reminder that the next generations should not allow such events to happen again.

The effect of the past on the present is made significant in the act of mourning for those who are lost through death, or through the end of a relationship. When Stephen traces the scar on Isabelle, for instance, their past love is invoked, but left in place. Their relationship is now consigned to history, but they both accept this.

Memories of events and people are also drawn upon to reiterate the importance of history, and it is implied that forgetting is impossible. Jack attempts to keep his thoughts of home separate from the war, and indeed the war almost takes over his memories of his son's face. However, his grief for John demonstrates that despite repressing or pushing aside such feelings, they still come back from the unconscious.

The lasting impact of the war is made concrete when Elizabeth visits Brennan in the nursing home he has been in for more than fifty years. The shame involved of forgetting the past is captured by the detail that he has not had a visitor for three decades. Without Elizabeth's intervention, or that of historians that research the past for those in the present, there is the chance that we will forget or remain ignorant. Through Elizabeth, then, Faulks makes the case for the importance of remembering and learning about what has come before.

THE ROLE OF WOMEN

Apart from the use of Elizabeth in the modern **narrative**, women function primarily as love interests for Stephen. This may be seen in the affair he has with Isabelle and in Lisette's flirtations, which

? QUESTION
Isabelle's scar may be interpreted as a **symbol** of the lasting damage of the war. How does this scar fit with other aspects of the novel that refer to body parts in relation to war and sex?

CHECK THE BOOK

Women's Writing on the First World War (1999), edited by Agnes Cardinal, Dorothy Goldman and Judith Hattaway, is an anthology that includes writing by Rebecca West, May Sinclair and Virginia Woolf.

he fends off. Jeanne is also portrayed as another woman who is attracted to him and demonstrates her affection by persuading him to continue to think of the future. Because these women are portrayed as adjuncts to his needs, Stephen's heroic, heterosexual central role is maintained and he is depicted as someone who cannot help but draw these women to him.

The passion and care shown by women appear essential, however, to Stephen's survival. This more complex aspect of their role is made clear by the part women play in their absence. Isabelle fits neatly into this category – her departure leaves such a void in Stephen's life that the war comes as a relief for him. Stephen's absent mother is also of importance because his loneliness is often explained in terms of her abandonment of him. In contrast, there is only one mention of his father.

Mothering, and the thought of being a mother, is another important part of the novel. Isabelle's concern for her unborn child, for example, is enough to make her leave Stephen with no explanation. In past centuries, mothering has been regarded as a role that women naturally desire to have, and without it they have been considered unnatural. With the advent of feminism in the 1970s, this stereotype has been challenged; however, such politics appear not to have influenced Elizabeth for being a mother becomes a major concern for her.

With Elizabeth, a gesture is made to the independence of women in the later twentieth century, but her concerns with domesticity are seen to run in tandem with her stated aim of trying to find out more about the past. Faulks says in his Introduction that he took the advice of his publishers to make her a character that offers 'a feminist example by being more successful in her business ...', thus sharpening the contrast between her life and the time that has gone before (p. xvii). Whether or not this stated intention has been brought to pass, perhaps demonstrates the potential pitfalls in allowing the author's intentions to influence our interpretations of the text.

LANGUAGE AND STYLE

There are differences between the language of Part One (1910) and the war sections primarily because of the differences in the subject matter. The style is more clipped, and this is achieved with the use of fewer adjectives and with a change in the use of verbs as Faulks explains in his Introduction: 'In the war sections, I tried to introduce an unstable feeling by various grammatical means, which included reducing the number of adjectives and increasing the number of active verbs' (p. xvi). This has the effect of increasing the pace, as is in keeping with scenes that are concerned with action, and it also maintains the **realism** of the **narrative**. The description of the attack on the Messines Ridge in Part Four is a good example of Faulks's intentions: '[Stephen] had to swerve over fallen bodies and leap small craters in the mud. He could see that the advancing line had reached the enemy trench' (p. 376).

The war scenes are united with Part One, however, by the constant stream of references to the body. These occur most significantly in the sex scenes between Isabelle and Stephen and to a lesser extent when he observes her or sits close to her (for example, when they are travelling on the boat and the train). The body is repeatedly described in terms of desire and death, and the two are linked together by this **motif**. This is confirmed when Isabelle takes Stephen's hand to help him trace the scar on her face. Here, her disfigured body bears the marks of war and a proximity to death, as well as a reference to their earlier passion (p. 336).

Such close-ups of the body and its functions, and the descriptions of what happens when the body is damaged beyond repair, are evoked in the service of realism. The numerous unflinching descriptions of the war dead and injured also mean that it is impossible for readers to escape from the trauma of war. When Stephen recovers from his life-threatening injuries in Part Two, he witnesses the suffering of a young man who has been injured by fire and poisoned gas: 'The soft skin on the armpits and inner thighs was covered in huge, raw blisters. He was breathing in short fast gasps' (p. 186). The narrative goes on to describe how he cannot bear to touch the sheets and cannot make a sound because of the damage incurred. The 'silent protest' he makes after being

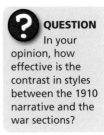

QUESTION
In your opinion, how effective is the contrast in styles between the 1910 narrative and the war sections?

pushed down on the bed by the doctor is evident only in the form of a 'yellow froth' that comes from his lips (p. 186). This scientific approach to the body is also used in the description of Stephen as he reinhabits his body 'cell by cell' in his recovery (p. 185). The **imagery** highlights how he comes back to life gradually, and emphasises how profoundly damaged he has been.

IMAGERY AND SYMBOLISM

Given the title and Stephen's phobia, birds and birdsong are a central **motif**. The horror, for Stephen, of the flapping of birds' wings is described in the telling of a recurring childhood dream. In this passage, there is a phrase that captures the panic he feels, as the imagined birds 'brought their beaks towards his face' and the threat they contain is made evident (p. 47). His phobia is most notable when he sits with Isabelle and reacts to the presence of a pigeon, and when he is forced to return the canary back to the trenches. These birds represent a form of primitivism that Stephen is not able to control or repress.

Birdsong is used traditionally to evoke innocence. Because of this, Stephen's horror is all the more noticeable and unexpected. The associations with birds are manifold, then, and Faulks draws on these multiple meanings to maintain an ambiguity. In terms of superstition, which Stephen and many of the soldiers at least partially adhere to, birds are often regarded as ill omens. Conversely, birds such as doves are inseparable from the concept of peace and hope, perhaps because of biblical references (for example, Noah and the discovery of land); and in poetry, such as Keats's 'Ode to a Nightingale', in which a bird is used to evoke an image of transcendence.

Furthermore, the sound of birds is constantly referred to throughout the novel and is often used to register the end of events: for example, after Stephen and Isabelle make love and when Stephen walks back to the British line at the end of the war. The birds can be heard when the noise of war stops; they fill the silence that is left. Their continuing sound implies that life continues despite tragedy.

CHECK THE POEM
Siegfried Sassoon's 'Everyone Sang' (1918) celebrates the signing of the Armistice and uses birdsong as an uplifting **metaphor**.

The novel ends with the 'ambiguous call' of a crow that can be heard 'by those still living' (p. 503). The ambiguity suggests the continued presence of nature despite subsequent wars, as well as the fear that Stephen felt. This strange note also exemplifies how complicated the **symbol** of the bird is, for Stephen and in the wider context.

An example of vivid imagery in *Birdsong* is the red room where Isabelle and Stephen have sex and the red room in the home of the prostitutes. The colour signifies danger and lust; it is also used to echo the blood that is lost in war. In relation to this, Isabelle refers to her periods as 'blood' (p. 35), confirming the interest this novel takes in the functions of the body. Blood is, of course, also referred to in the graphic accounts of the injuries the men receive: 'Douglas's blood had run up inside the arms of Stephen's uniform. It was on his face and in his hair. His trousers were saturated' (p. 156).

Religious imagery and symbolism are rife particularly when the men encounter the probability of death before they go into attack. They are depicted as taking Communion before the first day of the Battle of the Somme: believers and non-believers take part in the ritual. The men are seen to search for some comfort in this desperate time, as well as expressing a fraction of hope that they may be saved.

The parable of the Prodigal Son is invoked on several occasions and is used to highlight the theme of Christian-inspired forgiveness. By using a tenet of the New Testament, the spirit of Christianity rather than the institution is drawn upon to give characters such as Stephen and Jack hope. On a larger scale, its use forces us to consider the concept of unconditional, redemptive love.

The cross is a recognisable symbol of Christianity and is used tellingly. The padre throws his down as a mark that he questions his faith, and Jack is described as being attached to a wooden one while in the tunnels: 'His back was supported by a wooden cross, his feet against the clay, facing towards the enemy' (p. 121). This cross literally supports his back, but symbolically it signposts his faith and spirituality before they are diminished. By associating Jack with the cross, his worthiness and possible martyrdom are suggested.

CHECK THE POEM

Ted Hughes's *Crow: From the Life and Songs of the Crow* (1972), is a collection of dark and supernatural poems, which explore life, death and experience, via the mythic 'Crow'. Poems such as 'Crow's battle fury' and 'Crow's account of the battle' are strongly reminiscent of the more visceral imagery of *Birdsong*.

Burial is a significant emblem used to refer to various aspects of the lives of the men, as with the description of Stephen after Isabelle leaves him: 'Something had been buried that was not yet dead' (p. 161). It is also used literally when the men are buried alive or dead in the tunnels after explosions, and, of course, when they are formally buried after their bodies are recovered.

Faulks describes the urge to believe in superstition several times in the novel. Stephen is depicted as interested in at least the idea of fortune-telling when he first appears in 1910. The cards give him, and later Weir, a ritual to believe in and **symbolise** a hope in faith when everything else has dissolved. The sacrificed dead rat and candles that Stephen uses in his reading for Weir are a myth that he has created as he draws on and converts superstitious practices and beliefs for his own purposes.

QUESTION
Why is superstition important to the men in the war sections?

At times, the **narrative** colludes with this air of prophecy, lending some mystery to the novel. The 'piling up of the dead' that Stephen envisages in Amiens cathedral is the most memorable example of this. Furthermore, when Isabelle is pregnant she thinks of how sons in the area where she is living would only meet in a war (p. 110), and Weir has a premonition before his death (p. 373).

Because of the narrative drive that insists on there being the possibility of redemption despite the deaths of millions, Stephen develops an unnamed faith that, although not superstition *per se*, is not confined by religious institutions either. It has its roots in Christianity, as is demonstrated when he experiences 'binding love' and considers the possibility of redemption (p. 363). However, he does not seek out the approbation of others, as he explains to Jack in the tunnel in Part Six. This singlemindedness is also suggested symbolically in his embrace of the enemy (who is depicted in Levi) whom he has forced himself to hate for four years.

NARRATIVE TECHNIQUE

This war story, which is also a love story, has a third-person **narrator** throughout. This third-person voice is unobtrusive, providing the perspectives of several of the main characters as their thoughts and fears are revealed. This means that it is occasionally possible to see how different characters feel about shared circumstances. In Part One, for example, the perspectives of both Stephen and Isabelle are given just before she decides to leave him. Because the narrative switches from one point of view to the other it is explained how Stephen wants to tell Isabelle more about his past and show her his grandparents' home, and she is concerned that he is secretive about his earlier life. In this instance, Isabelle's thoughts are given via a letter she writes to Jeanne and so her first-person voice is recorded (pp. 114–16).

A realist style is used to convey events in the tradition of authors such as Flaubert. It is complemented by a movement between stories and time-frames, which is characteristic of more modern, even modernist, texts, and the most significant shift in the narrative comes with the jump forward in time from 1916 to 1978–9. This means that the linearity is spliced with alternate time-frames from Part Three onwards and has the obvious effect of demonstrating the links between the past and present. The effect is emphasised in the detail of Elizabeth being Stephen's granddaughter, but is also explored in the parallels between the past and present. The foremost of these is the continued theme of regeneration, and culminates when Elizabeth names her son John (for Stephen and Jack). Stephen and Elizabeth are also given some similar characteristics, such as their fear of tunnels and their desire for independence, thus linking them and the different times in which they live.

CHECK THE BOOK

Mrs Dalloway (1925) by Virginia Woolf is a modernist novel which, like *Ulysses* (1922) by James Joyce, is set on one day. In the **characterisation** of Septimus Smith, who is a victim of shell-shock, it reflects the impact of the war. Woolf's *Jacob's Room* (1921) is also concerned with the influence of the First World War.

PART FOUR

CRITICAL PERSPECTIVES

READING CRITICALLY

CHECK THE BOOK

Peter Barry's *Beginning Theory: An Introduction to Literary and Cultural Theory* (1995, 2002) is an excellent guide to those studying literary theory and shows students how to use it in relation to literary works.

This section provides a range of critical viewpoints and perspectives on *Birdsong* and gives a broad overview of key debates, interpretations and theories proposed since the novel was published. It is important to bear in mind the variety of interpretations and responses this text has produced, many of them shaped by the critics' own backgrounds and historical contexts.

No single view of the text should be seen as dominant – it is important that you arrive at your own judgements by questioning the perspectives described, and by developing your own critical insights. Objective analysis is a skill achieved through coupling close reading with an informed understanding of the key ideas, related texts and background information relevant to the text. These elements are all crucial in enabling you to assess the interpretations of other readers, and even to view works of criticism as texts in themselves. The ability to read critically will serve you well both in your study of *Birdsong*, and in any critical writing, presentation or further work you undertake.

CRITICAL RECEPTION

Writers have returned repeatedly to the First World War as a source of powerful subject matter. As an example of the **genre** of the **historical novel**, *Birdsong* has proved a very popular success. Because the novel was published in 1993, there is still only a comparatively small body of criticism associated with it. There are some notable reviews, however, and these are useful sources for the differing insights they give into this work.

The popularity of *Birdsong* has been established for a number of years and sales figures have been strong. It was voted thirteenth in the British nation's vote for the favourite 'Big Read', organised by the BBC in 2003. The novel had not been adapted for film as many of the entries were and yet was placed ahead of works such as *Great Expectations*, *Rebecca* and *Gone With the Wind*, so it is clear that *Birdsong* has been accepted into the national imagination.

Initial reviews were generally complimentary, but there were also criticisms. In *The New York Times*, Michael Gorra describes the scenes set in the tunnels and trenches as 'superb' and regards the prose in these sections as 'spare and precise'. He uses the example of the description of Weir being shot and praises it for the atmosphere it creates: 'It is as if Mr. Faulks had bled his own prose white, draining it of emotion in order to capture the endless enervating slog of war' (11 February 1996).

The title of Gorra's review is 'Tunnel Vision' and this indicates some of the criticisms he goes on to outline. Putting aside the war sections, he is troubled by what he calls the 'other two stories', that is, Part One that is set in 1910 and the sections involving Elizabeth. He interprets Stephen's affair with Isabelle as having 'little bearing on the war narrative proper' and because of this the third story set in the 1970s is never fully 'established'. He also interprets Elizabeth as too 'obtuse' to be believable, especially as the readers are expected to see her as 'intelligent and well educated', and for this reason he finds this part of the novel a disappointment (11 February 1996).

Writing for the *New Yorker*, Simon Schama points out that this may not be a perfect novel, but it is, for him, 'ambitious, outrageous, poignant, sleep-disturbing' (1 April 1996). In the *Kirkus Reviews*, *Birdsong* is described as such: 'The war, here, is Faulks's real subject, his stories of destroyed lives, however wrenching, only throwing its horror into greater relief and making it the more unbearable' (1 December 1995).

 CHECK THE BOOK
Raymond Williams's *Keywords* (1976) challenges the inferior status given to popular culture.

 CHECK THE BOOK
In his review, Michael Gorra discusses *Birdsong* in relation to Wilfred Owen's 'Strange Meeting'. He also compares the novel unfavourably with A. S. Byatt's *Possession* (1990) and refers to how both novels have scenes set in different times.

BIRDSONG AND CRITICAL MOVEMENTS

Critical theory gives students various frameworks to aid their analysis of a literary text. On a simplified level, Marxist theory engages with the process of history and class conflict. It looks to society and the way it is constructed, and challenges the inequalities that arise in a capitalist system. Key theorists who have developed the concepts of Karl Marx include Louis Althusser and Pierre Macherey. Feminist theory is also overtly political and generally speaking it questions the inequalities in society in terms of gender distinction. It criticises **patriarchal** dominance and points out that this is an abuse of power. It is a useful theory for examining representations of gender and the role of women and men in society. Psychoanalytic theory is developed from the ideas of psychoanalysts such as Sigmund Freud and Jacques Lacan. It is a helpful tool for discussing concepts such as repression and the fear of the loss of love. Students should take care, however, to avoid attempting to psychoanalyse the author and try not to make their interpretations too literal. This is a useful theory for examining the suggested implications of a text.

On a more complex level, it is necessary to point out for future research that many theorists are aware of the work of others and are influenced accordingly. Writers such as Hélène Cixous and Julia Kristeva use psychoanalysis in their work and also use feminist thinking and poststructuralist theory to shade their perspectives. Louis Althusser's work demonstrates an interest in psychoanalysis and poststructuralism as well as Marxism. Before understanding these ramifications, however, it is good to have at least a foundational understanding of the separate approaches and how they shed light on this text.

MARXISM

When interpreting the ways that class differences are depicted in a text, Marxism offers a framework and vocabulary to assist our analysis. The portrayal of Stephen is worth noting because of his central position in the **narrative**. Stephen's working-class background and promotion to staff during the war are vital aspects

CONTEXT

Louis Althusser (1918–90) is an influential twentieth-century Marxist theorist who drew on other schools of thought such as psychoanalysis and structuralism to explain the role of ideology in oppression.

of his character and the novel. His varied history allows him to have a freedom from the hierarchical class distinctions and enables the narrative to be more free-roaming than if he were more stereotypically working class or middle class. He spent his early childhood as a farm boy and after Vaughan became his guardian he was given the education of a middle-class boy of the period. He joined the army in the ranks and was promoted, and his education played a part in this. Through him, it is possible for different strata of British society to be depicted. That is, from a Marxist perspective this central character is relieved of the usual class boundaries in order to give the novel a broader remit.

Despite Stephen's relative freedom, *Birdsong* remains a work that is conscious of class and for the most part condemns the hypocrisy of the bourgeoisie, especially through the depictions of Azaire and Bérard. Their opposition to the strikers in Part One sits easily with the property-owning classes they represent and their individualism is challenged in the way they are both revealed to be misogynists. Furthermore, in Azaire's case there is a lack of care or responsibility for the plight of his workers, as is perceived by Stephen when Azaire bargains with Meyraux: 'He had made no pretence that the work force had anything to gain from the new arrangements or that they would make up in some other way for what they were clearly being asked to forgo' (p. 21).

There is also a running thread that critiques the strategists of the war, such as Haig, and is anti-establishment in its criticisms of the orders and planning. Althusser argued that members of society are controlled by obvious means such as the police and the army and by less obvious forms such as the media. *Birdsong* highlights how little control those serving in the war had over their own destinies and tends to show how this came about by direct means, as with the news that the men would be shot on the spot if they did not follow orders at the Battle of the Somme; however, it barely covers the influence of propaganda and peer pressure to join up and serve.

Using the same Marxist position, but looking at the novel in more negative terms, it is possible to ask if the narrative questions the ruling classes enough and if having the main focus on Stephen serves to limit the criticisms of the war and those who mismanaged

> **CONTEXT**
>
> Pierre Macherey (1938–) is a significant contributor to Marxist theory, in particular for his understanding of the 'significant silence' in a text, which generally speaking refers to the gaps in a text that reveal its ideology.

it. From this perspective, the affair with Isabelle may be construed as distracting us from the main narrative thread of war. The story involving Elizabeth takes us even further away from this subject because her concerns with pregnancy and symbolic renewal mean that the legacy of war is limited to her individual level. We could argue that it is only with the references to Brennan that the lasting damage is highlighted.

FEMINISM

Feminism has been strongly associated with the fight for women's rights and within this remit there has been, especially since the 1970s, a growing identification with the idea that 'the personal is political'. When compared generally to Marxism, for example, feminists have been mindful that the unequal distribution of power exists not only in the workplace, or the public sphere, but has also been elemental to the family and home, in the private sphere.

Under the umbrella of feminist theory, the challenge to fixed gender roles and the questioning of the notion that men should be masculine and women should be feminine has long been a predominant and unifying interest. There are many different feminist perspectives that vary in the focus they place, but they all tend to agree that men and women learn to be masculine and feminine respectively and those who do not conform to these roles are condemned in society for being so-called abnormal. Feminists see these roles as being prescribed rather than biological and Simone de Beauvoir's view in *The Second Sex* (1949) that 'one is not born a woman, one becomes one' is often cited as an explanation of this (and is quoted by Peter Barry in *Beginning Theory* (1995, 2002)).

 CHECK THE BOOK
Simone de Beauvoir's *The Second Sex* (1949) is a seminal feminist text that remains highly regarded in the twenty-first century.

Feminism is useful, therefore, for interpreting how *Birdsong* criticises the dominant view that men who fight in a war should be brave when walking into an almost certain death. By portraying the fears of the men before they go over the top, the stereotyped view of how a masculine man should behave is critiqued. Faulks demonstrates that masculinity is not a biological 'normality' but one that is imposed on men and is a restrictive way of understanding gender differences.

In a similar vein, Isabelle is expected to behave according to propriety: to be feminine and, therefore, acquiescent, in her acceptance of her husband's brutality. Before her affair with Stephen, she conforms to this expectation and remains faithful to Azaire. Isabelle's relationship with Stephen shows her finding a means of escape from this prescribed role, although it could be argued that she never does so fully because she never finds independence from the male partner. Given the context of the time in which the novel is set, however, this is both understandable and realistic.

Feminism is also useful for analysing how Elizabeth appears to resemble a modern woman in comparison to Isabelle but she is characterised as just as limited in her understanding of the choices she has. From a feminist perspective, it could be argued that Elizabeth and Isabelle differ mainly because Elizabeth runs her own company; apart from this Elizabeth has been barely touched by twentieth-century feminism. Depending on our point of view, we may regard this as a realistic touch on Faulks's part because his novel demonstrates the tenacity of patriarchy. Conversely, we may consider the novel's portrayal of Elizabeth as being limited by patriarchal thinking in that she is seen to be driven so powerfully by biology in the latter stages of the novel.

PSYCHOANALYTIC THEORY

The role of the unconscious and the idea of repression are key interests in psychoanalytic theory. Freud discussed how material experiences that are repressed, and so pushed down into the unconscious, always return. This may happen in dreams, 'Freudian slips' (unintentional revelations) and in the resurfacing of suppressed memories. The role of the parents is also a key feature of many psychoanalytic readings and is perhaps most famous in Freud's description of the Oedipus complex. This may offer a useful framework for analysing the relationship between mother and son or a love triangle in a work of literature, as well as the relationships between Stephen and Isabelle and Stephen and Jeanne.

In relation to this novel, repression may be compared to the **motif** of burial. Men are buried alive when there are explosions in the

CHECK THE BOOK

The Interpretation of Dreams (1900) is perhaps one of Sigmund Freud's best known works.

tunnels and as readers we observe the burial of the dead in several ceremonies. The construction of the tunnels under no-man's-land is also evocative of burial because of the claustrophobia they induce. Burial is a **metaphor** for repression as both are the means for covering over matter that never entirely disappears and it is fitting that this term is used to explain Stephen's emotions for Isabelle after she left him.

The use of the word 'fossil' to describe Stephen's horror of birds as well as his memory of Isabelle is another indication of repression because he has attempted, and failed, to forget both of these things (pp. 306 and 324 respectively). A fossil is a living reminder of the dead; its existence is a reminder of the past. Repression is also literally presented in Isabelle's relationship with Azaire. She performs her duties and behaves as expected until she has sex with Stephen, and with him she is seen to no longer repress the desires she has felt but never experienced.

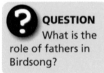

QUESTION
What is the role of fathers in Birdsong?

The desire for the love of the mother is one that resurfaces in the war sections and is most noticeable when the men are immediately threatened with death. Psychoanalysts such as Freud and Lacan often refer to the wish for a mother's love. Lacan has argued that we, as humans, never fully recover from the lost mother of our early infancy. Our separation is forever mourned and in *Birdsong* it is possible to see a re-enactment of this poignancy as, when near death, the men cry for the mother they lost years before. The scenes involving the tunnels may also be interpreted in this light as they offer the men a metaphoric return to this early state as they (**figuratively**) crawl back to the womb.

Stephen's love for the older more sophisticated woman is evident in his desire for Isabelle and his relationship with her and Jeanne. When using psychoanalytic theory, both women may be interpreted as a replacement of his lost mother. In the theory of the Oedipus complex, the son desires the mother; the son sees the father as a rival for her affections until he learns to identify with the father and move on to other relationships. It is worth noting that the care Jeanne shows for Stephen is especially resonant of the protective love a mother is expected to show for her son.

BACKGROUND

SEBASTIAN FAULKS'S LIFE AND WORKS

Sebastian Faulks was born near Newbury, England in 1953. He was educated at Wellington College and at Emmanuel College, Cambridge, where he studied English literature and graduated in 1974. His brother, Edward, to whom he dedicates *Birdsong*, is a barrister. His father, Peter Faulks, was a judge and was awarded the Military Cross during the Second World War. His mother, Pamela Faulks née Lawless, is the daughter of Philip Lawless who served in the First World War and was killed while reporting on the Second World War.

After graduating, Faulks worked as an editor for the book club, New Fiction Society. On leaving, he worked as a journalist at *The Daily* and *Sunday Telegraph* and in 1986 he was employed as the first literary editor of the *Independent*. He went on to become the deputy editor of the *Independent on Sunday* before he left in 1991 to commit to writing full-time.

His first novel, *A Trick of the Light* (1984), was barely acknowledged by the reading public, and although *The Girl at the Lion d'Or* (1989) fared well with reviewers, it did not achieve high sales. This was also the case with *A Fool's Alphabet* (1992), which uses the alphabet to structure its narrative. It was with *Birdsong* (1993) that Faulks achieved a breakthrough into the bestseller market and, although not an immediate success, it has gone on to sell in the millions.

Following *The Girl at the Lion d'Or* and *Birdsong*, *Charlotte Gray* (1998) marks the third novel in a trilogy that is connected with the use of France as a background. *Charlotte Gray* is set during the Second World War and the eponymous heroine is the daughter of Captain (then Colonel) Gray, who is Stephen's commanding officer in *Birdsong*; the novel was adapted as a film in 2001.

 CHECK THE BOOK

The Girl at the Lion d'Or (1989) is Faulks's first novel in what has come to be known as his French trilogy. It is set in France in 1936 and looks back to the influence of the past (the First World War) as well as giving a backdrop for the war to come.

The Fatal Englishman: Three Short Lives (1996) gives the life stories of Christopher Wood, Richard Hillary and Jeremy Wolfenden, who each live through various important events of the twentieth century, including the Battle of Britain and the Cold War. With *On Green Dolphin Street* (2001), Faulks marked a return to full-length fiction. *Human Traces* (2005) is regarded as thoroughly researched and is concerned with psychiatry. By contrast, *Engleby* (2007) shifts in tone and style as readers are exposed to the trajectory of lonely Cambridge student Mike Engleby from the 1970s on. On his official website, Faulks explains he had wanted to call the novel *Memoirs of a Jackass*, but was dissuaded from doing so by his agent and publisher. Faulks's well publicised James Bond novel *Devil May Care* was published in 2008 to mark the centenary of Ian Fleming's birth.

In recognition of his achievements, Faulks was elected as a Fellow of the Royal Society of Literature in 1993. He was named the 1994 British Book Awards Author of the Year, and *Charlotte Gray* was shortlisted for the James Tait Black Memorial Prize for Fiction in 1998. In 2002, Faulks was awarded the CBE for services to literature. He is married with three children.

CONTEXT

Faulks's engagement as the author of a new James Bond book, *Devil May Care* (2008), was given wide publicity and may be interpreted as a recognition of his popularity with the reading public.

LITERARY BACKGROUND

Birdsong follows primarily in the tradition of First World War literature, but it is also a romance and a story of what happens to a child who feels alone in the world. Because of its subject matter, it is by default a historical novel that highlights Faulks's ongoing interest in war in France.

THE FIRST WORLD WAR

The First World War has been a source of inspiration for numerous authors and artists both at the time and ever since. Works by poets such as Wilfred Owen, Siegfried Sassoon and Rupert Brooke chronicled the experiences of those taking part. Texts published in the late 1920s and early 1930s, such as *Goodbye to All That* (1929) by Robert Graves, evoke the period with the distance of over a decade of hindsight.

This war has continued to capture the imagination of the reading public and *Birdsong* is one of a cohort of texts that demonstrated this in the latter part of the twentieth century. Susan Hill's *Strange Meeting* (1971) and Pat Barker's *Regeneration* trilogy (1991–5) are just some of the well received examples.

FRENCH NOVELS

In the Introduction, Faulks describes himself as being 'indebted' to authors such as Stendhal, who wrote many works including *The Red and the Black* (1830), and Emile Zola, who is perhaps most famous for *Germinal* (1885) and his use of **naturalism**, rather than to Gustave Flaubert (p. xvi). The reference to Flaubert is an unspoken indication of how readers have compared *Birdsong* to *Madame Bovary* (1857). This no doubt is because they both describe the adulterous affair of a provincial French woman. Because of the geographical setting and the use of **realism**, there are echoes here of the work of all three writers.

ROMANCE

Novels concerned with romance in the First World War are not common. *A Farewell to Arms* (1929) by Ernest Hemingway is one of the exceptions. As with *Birdsong*, the danger of loving another in wartime is a central focus.

Putting the war aside, the similarities with *Madame Bovary* and its theme of doomed love resonate in a reading of *Birdsong*. The themes of broken relationships and unachieved happiness also feature in many of the novels of Thomas Hardy, for example *Tess of the D'Ubervilles* (1891) and *Jude the Obscure* (1895).

HISTORICAL NOVELS

The historical novel has been embraced as a genre by the reading public and it is possible that *Birdsong* has profited from this interest. Walter Scott's *Waverley* novels are often regarded as establishing a taste for this genre in the nineteenth century, which has continued ever since. More recently, works as varied as *True History of the Kelly Gang* (2001) by Peter Carey, *The Other Boleyn*

CHECK THE BOOK

Paul Fussell's *The Great War and Modern Memory* (1975) looks at memoirs and literature of the First World War period and the influence the war has had on literature.

CHECK THE BOOK

Stendhal's *The Red and the Black* (1830) is set in nineteenth-century France. Julien Sorel is the main protagonist who is comparable with Stephen in that education allows him to move up the social hierarchy.

HISTORICAL NOVELS continued

CONTEXT

The popularity of television programmes such as *Timewatch* (first aired in 1981), *A History of Britain* (2000) and *The Monarchy* (2004) attest to the viewing public's ongoing interest in history.

Girl (2001) by Philippa Gregory and *Sacred Hunger* (1992) by Barry Unsworth have had a wide readership.

Birdsong has a proximity to the present day in the shifts forward to the 1970s, but is for the most part a retrospective view of the war. The popularity of fiction concerned with past events could be linked with the more generalised interest in the subject of history (on television too). Furthermore, the awareness of the passing of time was heightened in the 1990s as the new millennium approached: the act of looking back to history, through interpretation, is an understandable response to the weight of time.

THE ORPHANED CHILD

The use of an orphan as a central **protagonist** is a long-standing feature in literature for adults and children. Although Stephen does not know if his parents are alive or not, he is depicted as being abandoned by those he loves and then removed from those who remain; he is alone in the world. This **trope** has been used by many authors such as Dickens and more recently J. K. Rowling to allow the hero of the piece, as a child, to be free to have adventures without parental constraint. Charlotte Brontë's *Jane Eyre* (1847) and William Faulkner's *Light in August* (1932) are two further examples of novels that have an orphaned child at the centre of the plot.

Parallels between Charles Dickens's *Great Expectations* (1861) and *Birdsong* are not immediately obvious because of the different settings and time of writing. However, the **characterisation** of Stephen as a child who receives help from a benefactor has similarities with Pip, as does the rejection of both Stephen and Pip by the women they love (Isabelle and Estella respectively).

HISTORICAL BACKGROUND

THE FIRST WORLD WAR

The origins for the First World War are both complex and there are various factors that contributed to both the beginning and the extent of it. Alliances that were established between European countries in the years leading up to the outbreak are often cited as magnifying its scale, as is the increased militarism of several European countries including Britain and Germany.

The assassination of Archduke Franz Ferdinand in Sarajevo on 28 June 1914 is often cited as the trigger, but the maintenance of alliances between different countries meant that once one country had declared war others followed. The Central Powers consisted of Germany, Austria–Hungary, Bulgaria and the Ottoman Empire; the Allies were France, Britain and Russia with the USA entering the war in 1917.

Britain entered the First World War on 4 August 1914 after Germany broke the Treaty of London by invading Belgium. The invasion took place because Germany had acted on the Schlieffen Plan. The plan meant that in the event of possible war on two fronts (against both France and Russia), a quick defeat of France should enable Germany to defend its Eastern Front more securely. This signalled a further escalation of the war as the 'domino effect' took hold.

Although leaders and the media thought the war would be over by Christmas, it went on for four years and became a war of attrition. The Western Front, the main setting for *Birdsong*, is synonymous with literally bogged-down trench warfare where the Allied and Central Powers rarely gained any ground.

The Battle of the Somme is a central part of the novel. It ran from 1 July to 13 November 1916. It is infamous for a massive loss of life – on the first day there were an unprecedented 58,000 casualties among British troops (one third were killed). During the whole battle, it has been estimated that there were 420,000 casualties in the British army, 500,000 in the German army and 200,000 in the French.

CONTEXT

The Battle of the Somme has come to epitomise the futility of the First World War. Although both sides experienced massive casualties, they remained in virtual deadlock.

SOCIAL BACKGROUND

The majority of the novel is set in France in the second decade of the twentieth century, in Amiens in 1910 and on the Western Front from 1916 to 1918. The relationship between Isabelle and Stephen begins tentatively – the sexual tension between them is described but not acted upon. The restraint shown by Isabelle shows her awareness of the constraints placed on her by society, due to her gender and class; it is noticeable when she tells Stephen to respect her 'position' when he comes to talk to her in the garden (p. 30). This is an authentic reaction given that divorce and adultery in this period were not at all socially acceptable. Faulks also emphasises that, in the tenets of her religion, adultery is a sin.

The sections set in the 1970s describe a more relaxed period. This is seen in particular in the portrayal of Elizabeth and her relationship with Robert. There is, however, an indication that this affair, which comes sixty years after that between Stephen and Isabelle, remains a complex relationship. Because of this, the parallels between grandfather and granddaughter are made more certain: both are depicted as suffering from being the third person in a triangulated relationship.

CONTEXT

In Britain, women were given the right to divorce on the same grounds as men in 1923 and could now divorce for adultery. Divorce first became legal in France in 1792 after the Revolution; it was abolished in 1816 but legalised again in 1884.

World events	Sebastian Faulks's life	Literary events
1914 (28 June) Archduke Franz Ferdinand, heir to the throne of the Austria–Hungary Empire, assassinated in Sarajevo; (28 July) Austria–Hungary declares war on Serbia; (1 August) Germany declares war on Russia; (3 August) Germany declares war on France; (4 August) Germany invades Belgium and Britain declares war on Germany		
1916 (1 July) First day of the Battle of the Somme; (18 November) end of the Battle of the Somme		
1917 (6 April) USA declares war on Germany; (29 April) mutiny breaks out in the French army		**1917–18** Publication of Siegfried Sassoon's anti-war poems in *The Old Huntsman* and *Counter-Attack*
1918 (11 November) Armistice signed at 11 minutes past 11 am		
1919 Treaty of Versailles signed		
		1920 Posthumous publication of Wilfred Owen's poems, edited by Siegfried Sassoon
		1921 Publication of Virginia Woolf's, *Jacob's Room*

World events	Sebastian Faulks's life	Literary events
		1929 Publication of Ernest Hemingway's *A Farewell to Arms*, Erich Maria Remarque's *All Quiet on the Western Front* and Robert Graves's *Goodbye to All That* (a memoir)
		1930 Publication of Frederic Manning's *Her Privates We*
		1933 Publication of Vera Brittain's *Testament of Youth* (a memoir)
1939–45 Second World War		**1940** Publication of W. H. Auden's *Another Time*, including 'September 1, 1939' which marks the outbreak of the Second World War
1950 Outbreak of the Korean War		
	1953 (20 April) Born in Berkshire, England	
		1961 Publication of Joseph Heller's *Catch-22*, describing the futility of war and using the Second World War as a backdrop
		1963 First performance of the stage musical *Oh! What a Lovely War* (adapted for film in 1969)
1965 Ground troops used in the Vietnam War		

World events	Sebastian Faulks's life	Literary events
	1966 Starts at Wellington College	
		1971 Publication of Susan Hill's *Strange Meeting*
	1970–4 At Emmanuel College, Cambridge	
	1979 Begins work for the *Daily Telegraph* as a junior reporter	
	1984 Publication of first novel, *A Trick of the Light*	
	1983–6 Works for the *Sunday Telegraph*	
	1986 Becomes literary editor for *The Independent*	
	1989 Publication of *The Girl at the Lion d'Or*	
1991 First Gulf War		**1991** Publication of Pat Barker's *Regeneration* (first in the trilogy)
1992–5 War in Bosnia	**1992** Publication of *A Fool's Alphabet*	
	1993 Publication of *Birdsong*; elected Fellow of the Royal Society of Literature	**1993** Publication of Pat Barker's *The Eye in the Door* (second in the trilogy)
		1995 Publication of Pat Barker's *The Ghost Road* (third in the trilogy)
	1996 Publication of *The Fatal Englishman: Three Short Lives*	
	1998 Publication of *Charlotte Gray*	
	2001 Release of film adaptation of *Charlotte Gray*; publication of *On Green Dolphin Street*	

World events	Sebastian Faulks's life	Literary events
	2002 Awarded the CBE	
2003 Invasion of Iraq by troops led by the USA and supported by Britain		
		2004 Publication of Andrea Levy's *Small Island*
	2005 Publication of *Human Traces*	2005 Publication of Sebastian Barry's *A Long, Long Way*
	2007 Publication of *Engleby*	
	2008 Publication of the James Bond novel, *Devil May Care*	

OTHER WORKS BY SEBASTIAN FAULKS

A Trick of the Light, 1984

The Girl at the Lion d'Or, 1989

A Fool's Alphabet, 1992

The Fatal Englishman: Three Short Lives, 1996

Charlotte Gray, 1998

The Vintage Book of War Stories (edited with Jorg Hensen), 1999

On Green Dolphin Street, 2001

Human Traces, 2005

Pistache, 2006

Engleby, 2007

Devil May Care, 2008

REVIEWS OF SEBASTIAN FAULKS'S WORK

Michael Gorra, *The New York Times*, 11 February 1996
   Author gives a mixed review, preferring the war scenes to those set in 1910 and 1978–9

Kirkus Reviews, 1 December 1995
   An effusive review that finds little fault

Simon Schama, *New Yorker*, 1 April 1996
   A complimentary review

Jules Smith, 'Sebastian Faulks', www.contemporarywriters.com
   A critical perspective of Faulks's writing as well as a short biography, listing work and prizes

LITERARY CRITICISM AND BACKGROUND READING

Adrian Barlow, *The Great War in British Literature*, Cambridge University Press, 2000
Looks at the influence of the First World War on literature

Peter Barry, *Beginning Theory: An Introduction to Literary and Cultural Theory*,
Manchester University Press, 1995 (new edition 2002)
An extremely useful text for students who are new to or uncertain about using literary
theory

Simone de Beauvoir, *The Second Sex*, Vintage, 1949 (new edition 1997)
A seminal feminist text that remains highly regarded in the twenty-first century

Paul Fussell, *The Great War and Modern Memory*, Oxford, 1975 (new edition 2000)
Looks at memoirs and literature of the period and considers the influence the war has had
on literature

Lyn MacDonald, *Somme*, Penguin, 1983 (new edition 1993)
Gives thorough details of the Battle of the Somme

John Peck and Martin Coyle, *Literary Terms and Criticism*, Palgrave Macmillan, 2002
A thorough and helpful text for literature students of any level

Raymond Williams, *Keywords*, Fontana Press, 1976 (new edition 1988)
A complex work, but one of Williams's more accessible texts that assists in an
understanding of Marxist perspectives

FIRST WORLD WAR LITERATURE

ANTHOLOGIES

Agnes Cardinal, Dorothy Goldman and Judith Hattaway (eds), *Women's Writing on the
First World War*, Oxford University Press, 1999

Ian Parsons (ed.), *Men Who March Away*, Chatto & Windus, 1965

Catherine Reilly (ed.), *Scars Upon My Heart*, Virago, 1981 (new edition 2006)

DRAMA

George Bernard Shaw, *Heartbreak House*, 1919

MEMOIRS

Alan Bishop and Mark Bostridge (eds), *Letters from a Lost Generation*, 1998

Robert Graves, *Goodbye to All That*, 1929

NOVELS

Ernest Hemingway, *A Farewell to Arms*, 1929

Erich Maria Remarque, *All Quiet on the Western Front*, 1929

Virginia Woolf, *Jacob's Room*, 1921

POEMS

Thomas Hardy, 'Men Who March Away', 1914

Siegfried Sassoon, 'Everyone Sang', 1918

Siegfried Sassoon, 'Suicide in the Trenches', 1918

Siegfried Sassoon, 'The Dug-Out', 1919

LITERATURE ABOUT THE FIRST WORLD WAR

William Allison and John Fairley, *The Monocled Mutineer*, 1979

Pat Barker, *Regeneration*, 1991

Pat Barker, *The Eye in the Door*, 1993

Pat Barker, *The Ghost Road*, 1995

Sebastian Barry, *A Long, Long Way*, 2005

Susan Hill, *Strange Meeting*, 1971

Joan Littlewood, *Oh! What a Lovely War*, 1963

OTHER COMPARATIVE TEXTS

W. H. Auden, 'Miss Gee', 1937

Robert Browning, 'My Last Duchess', 1842

A. S. Byatt, *Possession*, 1990

Charles Dickens, *Great Expectations*, 1861

Gustave Flaubert, *Madame Bovary*, 1857

Sigmund Freud, *Beyond the Pleasure Principle*, 1920

Thomas Hardy, 'The Darkling Thrush', 1900

James Joyce, *The Dubliners*, 1914

James Joyce, *Ulysses*, 1922

Andrea Levy, *Small Island*, 2004

Ian McEwan, *Atonement*, 2001

Henry Newbolt, 'Vitae Lampada', 1897

Virginia Woolf, *Mrs Dalloway*, 1925

FILMS AND TELEVISION

Gillian Armstrong, *Charlotte Gray*, 2001

Richard Curtis and Ben Elton, *Blackadder Goes Forth*, 1989

Lewis Milestone, *All Quiet on the Western Front*, 1930

Simon Schama, *A History of Britain*, 2000

allegory a story or a situation with two different meanings: the straightforward meaning on the surface is used to symbolise a deeper meaning underneath, which might be a spiritual or moral one whose values are represented by specific figures, characters or events in the narrative

allusion a passing reference in a work of literature to something outside the text; may include other works of literature, myth, historical facts or biographical detail

characterisation the construction of a character brought about by such means as description, dialogue and background information

dialect a variety of speech, usually associated with geographical location, rather than social status; dialect covers vocabulary and syntax; accent covers the sound of the speech

dramatic irony when the implications of an episode or a speech are better understood by the audience than the characters

exposition introduction and explanation of events and character

figurative figurative language is distinguishable from literal language; it uses metaphors, similes and other such devices

genre literally means 'type'; in literary studies this refers to the classification of the work

historical novel a novel set in a time period prior to the time in which the author wrote it, in which the cultural/social/political events of that period play a significant part in the story

imagery descriptive language which uses images to make actions, objects and characters more vivid in the reader's mind; metaphors and similes are examples of imagery

irony the humorous or sarcastic use of words to imply the opposite of what they normally mean; incongruity between what might be expected and what actually happens; the ill-timed arrival of an event that had been hoped for

metaphor a figure of speech in which a word or phrase is applied to an object, a character or an action which does not literally belong to it, in order to imply a resemblance and create an unusual or striking image in the reader's mind

motif a small recurring idea in a work, which is used to draw the reader's attention to a particular theme or topic

LITERARY TERMS

narrative a story, tale or any recital of events, and the manner in which it is told. First-person narratives ('I') are told from the character's perspective and usually require the reader to judge carefully what is being said; second-person narratives ('you') suggest the reader is part of the story; in third-person narratives ('he', 'she', 'they') the narrator may be intrusive (continually commenting on the story), impersonal or omniscient. More than one style of narrative may be used in a text

narrator the voice telling the story or relating a sequence of events

naturalism takes the depiction of reality further than realism in reflecting not just life as it is (realism) but the conditions which created it

patriarch, patriarchy The *Oxford English Dictionary* defines the word 'patriarch' as 'a male head or ancestor of any people, tribe, or family'; patriarchy is a social system of government in which power is held by elder males and passed to the younger males exclusively

personification the treatment or description of an object or an idea as human, with human attributes and feelings

prolepsis the foreshadowing of events in the narrative

protagonist the principal character in a work of literature

realism realist texts aim to be realistic rather than overly idealised

satire a work in which folly, evil or topical issues are held up to scorn through ridicule, irony or exaggeration

simile a figure of speech which compares two things using the words 'as' or 'like'

symbolism investing material objects with abstract powers and meanings greater than their own; allows a complex idea to be represented by a single object

theme a principal and recurring aspect of a novel, play or poem, drawing together events, characters and ideas

tragedy in its original sense, a drama dealing with elevated actions and emotions and characters of high social standing in which a terrible outcome becomes inevitable as a result of an unstoppable sequence of events and a fatal flaw in the personality of the protagonist. More recently, tragedy has come to include courses of events happening to ordinary individuals that are inevitable because of social and cultural conditions or natural disasters

trope form of words or expression which is repeated for a particular effect

AUTHOR OF THESE NOTES

Julie Ellam has a PhD in English Literature and previously taught in the English
Department at the University of Hull for a number of years. She currently works as a
freelance writer and researcher.

GCSE

Maya Angelou
I Know Why the Caged Bird Sings

Jane Austen
Pride and Prejudice

Alan Ayckbourn
Absent Friends

Elizabeth Barrett Browning
Selected Poems

Robert Bolt
A Man for All Seasons

Harold Brighouse
Hobson's Choice

Charlotte Brontë
Jane Eyre

Emily Brontë
Wuthering Heights

Brian Clark
Whose Life is it Anyway?

Robert Cormier
Heroes

Shelagh Delaney
A Taste of Honey

Charles Dickens
David Copperfield
Great Expectations
Hard Times
Oliver Twist
Selected Stories

Roddy Doyle
Paddy Clarke Ha Ha Ha

George Eliot
The Mill on the Floss
Silas Marner

Anne Frank
The Diary of a Young Girl

William Golding
Lord of the Flies

Oliver Goldsmith
She Stoops to Conquer

Willis Hall
The Long and the Short and the Tall

Thomas Hardy
Far from the Madding Crowd
The Mayor of Casterbridge
Tess of the d'Urbervilles
The Withered Arm and other Wessex Tales

L. P. Hartley
The Go-Between

Seamus Heaney
Selected Poems

Susan Hill
I'm the King of the Castle

Barry Hines
A Kestrel for a Knave

Louise Lawrence
Children of the Dust

Harper Lee
To Kill a Mockingbird

Laurie Lee
Cider with Rosie

Arthur Miller
The Crucible
A View from the Bridge

Robert O'Brien
Z for Zachariah

Frank O'Connor
My Oedipus Complex and Other Stories

George Orwell
Animal Farm

J. B. Priestley
An Inspector Calls
When We Are Married

Willy Russell
Educating Rita
Our Day Out

J. D. Salinger
The Catcher in the Rye

William Shakespeare
Henry IV Part I
Henry V
Julius Caesar
Macbeth
The Merchant of Venice
A Midsummer Night's Dream
Much Ado About Nothing
Romeo and Juliet
The Tempest
Twelfth Night

George Bernard Shaw
Pygmalion

Mary Shelley
Frankenstein

R. C. Sherriff
Journey's End

Rukshana Smith
Salt on the snow

John Steinbeck
Of Mice and Men

Robert Louis Stevenson
Dr Jekyll and Mr Hyde

Jonathan Swift
Gulliver's Travels

Robert Swindells
Daz 4 Zoe

Mildred D. Taylor
Roll of Thunder, Hear My Cry

Mark Twain
Huckleberry Finn

James Watson
Talking in Whispers

Edith Wharton
Ethan Frome

William Wordsworth
Selected Poems

A Choice of Poets

Mystery Stories of the Nineteenth Century including The Signalman

Nineteenth Century Short Stories

Poetry of the First World War

Six Women Poets

For the AQA Anthology:

Duffy and Armitage & Pre-1914 Poetry

Heaney and Clarke & Pre-1914 Poetry

Poems from Different Cultures

Key Stage 3

William Shakespeare
Much Ado About Nothing
Richard III
The Tempest

Margaret Atwood
Cat's Eye
The Handmaid's Tale

Jane Austen
Emma
Mansfield Park
Persuasion
Pride and Prejudice
Sense and Sensibility

Pat Barker
Regeneration

William Blake
Songs of Innocence and of Experience

The Brontës
Selected Poems

Charlotte Brontë
Jane Eyre
Villette

Emily Brontë
Wuthering Heights

Angela Carter
The Bloody Chamber
Nights at the Circus
Wise Children

Geoffrey Chaucer
The Franklin's Prologue and Tale
The Merchant's Prologue and Tale
The Miller's Prologue and Tale
The Pardoner's Tale
The Prologue to the Canterbury Tales
The Wife of Bath's Prologue and Tale

Caryl Churchill
Top Girls

John Clare
Selected Poems

Joseph Conrad
Heart of Darkness

John Donne
Selected Poems

Charles Dickens
Bleak House
Great Expectations
Hard Times

Carol Ann Duffy
Selected Poems
The World's Wife

George Eliot
Middlemarch
The Mill on the Floss

T. S. Eliot
Selected Poems
The Waste Land

Sebastian Faulks
Birdsong

F. Scott Fitzgerald
The Great Gatsby

John Ford
'Tis Pity She's a Whore

John Fowles
The French Lieutenant's Woman

Michael Frayn
Spies

Charles Frazier
Cold Mountain

Brian Friel
Making History
Translations

William Golding
The Spire

Thomas Hardy
Jude the Obscure
The Mayor of Casterbridge
The Return of the Native
Selected Poems
Tess of the d'Urbervilles

Nathaniel Hawthorne
The Scarlet Letter

Homer
The Iliad
The Odyssey

Khaled Hosseini
The Kite Runner

Aldous Huxley
Brave New World

Henrik Ibsen
A Doll's House

James Joyce
Dubliners

John Keats
Selected Poems

Philip Larkin
High Windows
The Whitsun Weddings and Selected Poems

Ian McEwan
Atonement

Christopher Marlowe
Doctor Faustus
Edward II

Arthur Miller
All My Sons
Death of a Salesman

John Milton
Paradise Lost Books I and II

George Orwell
Nineteen Eighty-Four

Sylvia Plath
Selected Poems

William Shakespeare
Antony and Cleopatra
As You Like It
Hamlet
Henry IV Part I
King Lear
Macbeth
Measure for Measure
The Merchant of Venice
A Midsummer Night's Dream
Much Ado About Nothing
Othello
Richard II
Richard III
Romeo and Juliet
The Taming of the Shrew
The Tempest
Twelfth Night
The Winter's Tale

Mary Shelley
Frankenstein

Richard Brinsley Sheridan
The School for Scandal

Bram Stoker
Dracula

Alfred Tennyson
Selected Poems

Alice Walker
The Color Purple

Virgil
The Aeneid

John Webster
The Duchess of Malfi
The White Devil

Oscar Wilde
The Importance of Being Earnest
The Picture of Dorian Gray
A Woman of No Importance

Tennessee Williams
Cat on a Hot Tin Roof
The Glass Menagerie
A Streetcar Named Desire

Jeanette Winterson
Oranges Are Not the Only Fruit

Virginia Woolf
To the Lighthouse

William Wordsworth
The Prelude and Selected Poems

Wordsworth and Coleridge
Lyrical Ballads

Poetry of the First World War